JUST WORDS?

SPECIAL REVELATION AND THE BIBLE

PAUL HELM

EP Books (Evangelical Press), Registered Office: 140 Coniscliffe Road, Darlington, Co Durham DL3 7RT

admin@epbooks.org

www.epbooks.org

EP Books are distributed in the USA by:

JPL Books, 3883 Linden Ave. S.E., Wyoming, MI 49548

order@jplbooks.com

www.jplbooks.com

British Library Cataloguing in Publication Data available

ISBN 978-1-78397-197-8

For Bethan Hunter

CONTENTS

PREFACE

This short book is an attempt to link up the distinctive properties of the Christian view of special revelation, its classical properties of inspiredness and infallibility, to the place of the Bible in the life of faith in Christ. There are books which set forth this view more systematically: for example, J.I. Packer, *God has Spoken* (Hodder & Stoughton, 1979), and his earlier *'Fundamentalism' and the Word of God* (IVP, 1958), Timothy Ward, *Words of Life,* (IVP, 2009) and my own effort, *Revelation: The Basic Issues,* (1982, reprinted 2004, Regent College Publishing). Standing behind and above all these is the sterling work of B.B. Warfield, the articles gathered together in *Revelation and Inspiration,* (O.U.P., New York, 1937).

Thanks to Peter Sanlon for suggesting the book and providing the title, and for the help of Graham Hind.

Paul Helm

1. WHAT SORT OF BOOK IS THE BIBLE?

Which way does the arrow point? How do we begin to understand the Bible? Strange questions with which to begin a book on the Bible. But it is vital that from the start we understand the question correctly, and offer the correct answer. The wrong answer, and we lose our way. If when we think of 'religion', or 'the Christian religion' we think of a 'search' or of an 'exploration', then we are pointing the arrow the wrong way. Christianity is not the outcome of humankind's search for God, nor is the Old Testament an account of Israel's search for him. So if from the start we point the arrow from ourselves upward, pointing to the results of a search, trying to find God, then we shall quickly get into a tangle.

No, not upwards, but the search of the arrow points in the opposite direction. Not downwards, to the human race on planet Earth, and to its need. It signals the importance of three words, *God comes down*. It may help to keep these words in mind in what follows. Think of the arrow as indicating the way that God first of all acts. He comes down to us, coming to us to reveal the way to return to God, the only way. But where does God come down from? Down from beyond our universe existing in time and space, down from what is referred to as 'his own glory'.

God is *above* this universe, his creation. Though it is immeasurably great, he *transcends* it. But he comes down to it. That's quite a leap! We find this hard to grasp because we are used to thinking in exclusively spatial, physical terms. In coming down God does surprising things. He prepares himself for our company. He appears in visions and in dreams. He makes covenants. He acts in mercy and in judgment. He talks through his servants the prophets. In all this, what he says surprises men and women. 'Long ago, in many times and in many ways, God spoke to our fathers the prophets, but in these last days he has spoken to us by his Son...' (Hebrews 1.1) He is a surprising God, who routinely does the unexpected. And at the climax of this business, he comes down in the person of his Son, putting on our human nature, to make known his love, and to deliver us from what holds us captive. As John says, it is not as if we loved God, but that he loved us.

But the odd thing is this. According to the Bible, if we read it discerningly, we'll see that he comes down to us in modest ways. Though he is our Creator and Lord, the

King of Kings, when he comes to us, he adopts a sort of disguise. He does not come as a King, or at least not at all like the kings of the earth, or the Presidents, the Chancellors, the Prime Ministers, or the Chief Executives, who rule us. He comes in 'weakness', in everyday ordinariness, in humility. Only occasionally do those he comes to see shafts of his glory. This is one of the characteristics of God as he has appeared to us. He comes not to blind us, but to engage us. God in Christ woos his Bride.

WHAT THIS BOOK IS ABOUT

In this short book we are to consider one important aspect of the ordinariness with which God visits us. God has done things for us and he says things to us. Some of the things he does are to attract attention. But not like Presidents may command our attention, by their residence or their motorcade or the eloquence of their speech or the might of their army or the size of their entourage. In making himself known, God does not lose anything of his glory, but in what he does his glory shows through in surprising ways. And when all his redemptive work is done, his full glory will be manifest to all. Christ will come in great glory, and all his holy angels with him.

We learn that in God's dealings with the human race, *matter* and *manner* are intertwined, vitally connected. In this study we are considering God's book, what we call

The Holy Bible. It is a book made up of other books, spanning hundreds of years. This shelf of books itself has a character that is at one with God's coming down. For what God says in his book and how he says it are seamlessly woven together. The Bible tracks what has happened in human history when God came down.

TWO ELEMENTS

What do I mean? Basically, that the Bible is made up of two elements. There is a record of God's action. And there is a commentary on that action. Act plus commentary. When we hear of commentaries, we might think of journalists who take a line on current affairs, or of pundits who make remarks on what is going on during the match. The commentator is in the studio, and he talks about the game. But this is not how it is with the Bible. God is not simply a talker. The power and authenticity of the Bible lies in the fact that it is the record of actions of God *together with his own authoritative commentary on those actions*. The Bible is not a record of the acts of God with a commentary from some other source. God is his own commentator. This gives to the Bible an enduring relevance.

One view used to be that Bible is the record of how the people of Israel tried to make sense of the acts of God, developing a religion in doing so. But that's to reverse the arrow, I'm afraid. There are events − God coming down - and the human divinely-provided commentators, like Isaiah or the Apostle Paul, are part of the total event. There is the event itself and then what we may call a God-authorized commentary on that event. The Bible itself does not say this in so many words, but this is what is borne in on us when we start to study it carefully. This needs a word or two of further explanation.

If you watch a wordless video with some of your friends, and then discuss what its significance is, you are likely to get various reactions, some of which may be wildly different from others. Why was the man walking down the street into the sunset? Who was he? Where was he? And so on. Words, that is, sentences of various kinds, are needed to deliver intelligibility. That is the job of a commentator.

In the Bible there are various kinds of divine commentary. Some are very direct: the word of the Lord is said to 'come to' the prophets (see for example Jeremiah 1:2). Others are more reflective, through God's action. In such commenting there is a kind of dual authorship. In this situation. God acts, and then later—but sometimes before!—commentators act by speaking. God gives his words to the prophet. Perhaps they come to the prophet in a dream, or in an act of divine authorization. In speaking God does not only 'own' what he says. More than that, God so orders the details of the human agent's life that when he speaks, the distinctives of what he says are evident. Or if he is a scribe the style of what he has

written is like an official document, in which the character
of the writer is shielded from us. Several of the Old
Testament books of history, such as 1 and 2 Chronicles,
are like that. They might have been put together by a
committee. Otherwise as we read the Bible we see that
Paul is not Peter, and it shows. Isaiah is not Jeremiah.
Matthew is not John. Style and temperament and outlook
become manifest. God 'respects' the person's individuality
(after all, he has created and sustains him). He does not
'flatten' their individuality into a sort of monotone. The
prophet or apostle is not a puppet or simply one who
mouths God's words like a megaphone. Paul, for example,
speaks them out, the words bearing the stamp of his
personality, his education, his thought-processes, and so
on. Yet his words are the words of God. Sometimes the
message is given to the human agent to deliver is an
unwelcome one. He'd rather not say what he is divinely
impelled to say, but it has to be said.

Through this in-breathing of God the prophet's words
are not only his words, they are God's words. What the
exact mechanism of this is like it is difficult to say, since it
is the action of our Creator upon his creation, unlike any
human-on-human action. So the idea of 'dictation' doesn't
quite do the job of what is going on, not usually. When he
wrote his letters Paul was not 'dictated to' as in the old
days when the boss used to dictate a letter to his
secretary. At least, Paul's letters—or Luke's narratives—
don't read like that, do they?

Think of the well-known story of the young man Samuel. The Lord called to him during the night, but Samuel was at first convinced that it was the high priest Eli who was calling, and went to see what Eli wanted. After this had happened a few times, Eli came to the conclusion that it must be the Lord calling, and told Samuel that if it happened again he should say 'Speak, Lord, for your servant hears'. And the Lord spoke, and stated that he was going to punish Eli's two worthless sons, priests and yet blasphemers (1 Samuel 3).

Of course the process of bringing the story of Samuel into a history book of the people of Israel is not complete until that book is complete, and that involves another agent, or set of agents, who see to it that this story comes together with other stories of God's action and commentary, into the form of the book that we know as 1 Samuel. In fact you may say the process is not fully completed until that book takes its place in the library of books that make up the Bible. But we must not suppose that the agents—prophets and poets and scribes and compilers of sets of proverbs—have to be conscious of God's special agency for this to happen. The historians, say, need only to be conscious of being historians of Israel. Their role, as distinct from that of the prophet, is more like that of a sub-editor than that of an author. This process is also held to be under the superintendence of God, a rather different process than that of the direct inspiration of a prophet. A scribe works among the annals of the people, helping to form one of the sacred books such as the histories of the Old Testament, for example Judges or the books of Samuel.

In the case of Paul's letters the process was rather different, more informal, more personal, but written with an awareness of his apostleship (1 Corinthians 9:1). The letters may be said, in general, to be comments on the significance of what Jesus Christ did and said and suffered, how his readers should conduct themselves as the people of God, and so on. The letters are affectionate, personal, profound, and plain-speaking. They seem to have been composed in the ordinary way of writing letters, sometimes with a secretary, and (as far as the text indicates) sometimes not. Yet Paul so thought and wrote or dictated that what he produced was inspired by God.

This process of commenting is described in general in the opening words of the Letter to the Hebrews cited earlier. Here the writer draws attention to a whole historical chain of action and commentary culminating in the prophetic work of the Son of God, the one through whom the universe was created and who upholds what he has created.

DIVINE AGENCY

Can we explain this two-foldness, the agency of God and the agency of a series of human agents? No, not precisely. It is one of those types of event when God engages directly with the human agent as he does in the Incarnation and in the Creation out of nothing, for example. Each is unparalleled in our experience. We can say what they are *not* like better than we can say what they are like. I have been stressing that very different activities are involved in this, and so it would be unwise to make hasty generalizations as to what the process was.

This two-fold agency of preparing spoken material and comments and editorial finessing that were in due course written down is called *inspiration*, sometimes *plenary* inspiration, to underline the fact that God does not merely suggest something to Paul, say, and then leave Paul to put it unaided into his own words. It is not that God puts Paul into a certain mood and then leaves the rest to him. Sometimes one word, even one letter, makes a big difference. An interesting case of this is in Galatians. Writing about God's promise to Abraham, Paul writes:

Now the promises were made to Abraham and to his offspring. It does not say 'offsprings' referring to many, but referring to one. 'And to your offspring.'

— GALATIANS 3:16

In the course of his life Abraham had a considerable number of offspring, but the promise was made to him and only one of them, singular. Who was that? Paul says it referred to Christ, an offspring who lived many centuries after Abraham. Incidentally, this is an example of one of the important and distinctive features of Scripture. This is the fact that although the main figures in the New Testament (notably Christ himself in his spoken words, but also Paul and the other apostles) commented in various ways, nevertheless their work is harmonious and consistent. The result is that although the Bible is a shelf of books, it is nevertheless one self-interpreting document. More on this idea of self-interpretation in the next chapter.

REVELATION

This entire business we may call God's *revelation*, and the commentary side of things, the *inspiration* of God, which does not help us as to the exact manner. This is not the only revelation, for the natural world reveals the power and wisdom of God (Romans 1:19f.) This is called *general revelation*, and that which is recorded in the Bible is *special revelation*. This activity that we have been describing is said to be by the agency of the Holy Spirit, as in 'all scripture is breathed out by God' (2 Timothy 3:16). Somewhat similar but more explicit is the statement 'no prophecy was ever produced by the will of man, but men spoke from God as they were carried along by the Holy Spirit' (2 Peter 1:21). But what precisely these terms mean, or whether they are umbrella terms covering various phenomena, is not clear, except that they refer to the Spirit's direct activity.

It is possible to imagine revelation taking different forms, of having lesser degrees or kinds of divine-human agency. God's revelation might have taken the form of an oral human history, or of divine acts with a merely human commentary, for example. But in his wisdom God has chosen to reveal himself by himself acting and speaking and commenting through his agents, and by giving the result a permanent, written form. We shall consider this aspect, called the Canon or rule of Scripture, later on. This is how the arrow operates. In God coming down to us we are given the direction of things. The first idea is not that we speak, or invent a 'model' of 'the God we want,' but that God himself discloses matters about himself.

In the story of Samuel the Lord 'came and stood' with Samuel after he had called to the boy the third time, and when the bemused Samuel had responded as Eli had advised him (1 Samuel 3:10). This is not a direct word from the Lord but is a comment of a different kind, informing us of the setting. I wonder by what means that detail came to be in the text?) But it is an amazing detail. God stands by. How can that be? Not literally, because God has no feet nor is he enclosed within space and time. So it is as if he was standing, his message is fixed and steady, and his presence was such that he felt near. That is, he made himself so palpable to the puzzled Samuel that he concludes that he was like a man standing there.

The Bible is a very varied book, with much detail, the product of many centuries and by a variety of authors and in different genres of writing. So in trying to understand it, it would be unwise to flatten it out. But one dominant or recurrent feature is that in coming down to us God makes himself available to us. Not that we can experience him as Samuel did, but that in what he says and does, his concern is to make his character known to us. This is not merely to satisfy our curiosity. There is much that he has not revealed and perhaps much that he could not reveal, since our finite minds would not be able to take it in. In fact some of what he *has* revealed has this character. And all of what he has revealed has the oblique and off-centre manner that was mentioned earlier. Some students of the Bible call this God's 'accommodation.'

Let us think a little more about this. I have been stressing features of this divine activity some of which are ordinary. While the King of Heaven does come down, he rarely does that in a display of outward majesty. Instead he comes to men and women using the agency of a variety of men and women, or of a natural occurrence such as a cloud or a fire or thunder. There is not usually any outward show. When miracles occur, for example, they are often to signal a change. We can think of the calls of Abraham, the father of the faithful, and of Moses as the leader of his people out of Egypt, accompanied with signs.

The words to Samuel marked the beginning of a new era when the chaos recorded in Judges was to be dealt with by the establishment of a kingdom. The call of the persecutor Saul of Tarsus to be an apostle was similarly dramatic.

Among the most dramatic of all was the baptism of Jesus, a striking event as his Father announced and authorized the start of the ministry of his beloved Son, who healed the sick and demon-possessed.

THE EVERYDAY SIDE OF THINGS

There is another side to the forming of the Bible which you may have noticed and taken for granted. This is the important fact that the business of the making of the Bible is enmeshed in the ordinary events of human activity and history.

Perhaps as you are reading this book you have a copy of the Bible near at hand. In appearance it is like most other books. It has a table of contents, pages and paragraphs and chapters, maybe a concordance. A little research shows us that the words we read when we pick it up are translated from one language or another, largely from Hebrew in the Old Testament and from Greek in the New, into some style of English, or French or Swahili. Some people have learned these languages and done the translation work. They have had the help of grammars and dictionaries.

An important, everyday characteristic of God's special revelation, which is taken largely for granted, is that it used everyday language and discourse: Hebrew, Greek and bits of Aramaic. No 'language of heaven' was used which needed a special initiation into, as in Mystery Religions and those groups influenced by Gnosticism. The way of communicating the gospel is by words, words of Scripture and spoken words which, using other words, then faithfully presents the content of Scripture. As used to be said, the meaning of Scripture is Scripture.

Why stress these obvious points? Partly because they underline the important fact that Christianity is a public religion in the most obvious way. The mighty acts of God that Scripture records, strange and unique as they are, occurred in space and time, in locations in various places. When Paul, a prisoner on his way to Rome, was addressing the Roman governor Festus, he reminded him that his own conversion to Christ and the suffering, death and resurrection of Jesus were events that were not 'done in a corner' (Acts 26:26). They were public events, they had witnesses, and were proclaimed out loud. The events recorded and the method of their publicity are ordinary methods. The Christian gospel has nothing to hide. It is not in the hands of a special priesthood using a special 'religious' language all of its own. It was a definite step backward when the medieval church used Latin in worship and not the vernacular.

To become joined to the Christian church people do

not have to undergo elaborate processes of initiation. The message is usually spread through people speaking to other people, and so by the straightforward business of hearing and reading. The process of translation, which is a necessary stage in this, is fully in accord with some of the last words of Jesus, that his first disciples were to take the good news to all the nations of the world. Christ is an international Saviour, and the Bible is an international book. Christianity is not a 'a mystery religion' full of hocus-pocus. It is not mumbo jumbo. But we do need to read, or hear, in order to understand it.

Though this may seem to be an obvious point, the apostles stress it. John says that Jesus was heard and seen and touched (1 John 1:1 f.); the five senses were enough to locate him and to learn from him. The only obstacles are found within us, like the slowness of heart of the disciples whom Jesus met incognito after his resurrection, on the road from Jerusalem to Emmaus (Luke 24:25). No one needs the addition of a sixth sense. Why not? Because when God was incarnated in Jesus Christ, the body was one of flesh and blood. Though he had a miraculous birth it was to a natural mother that he was born. In a similar way to John, Peter describes himself as an 'eyewitness of his (Christ's) majesty, hearing a voice from the Majestic Glory'—he is referring to the Transfiguration, and to the 'sure word of prophecy' that comments on it and endorses it.

WORDS AND THE WORD

This stress on the *words* of the Bible is sometimes misunderstood. Those who misunderstand give the impression that this focus on the linguistic detail of Scripture somehow gets in the way. 'In my need I am seeking the help and assurance of God and you keep talking about a book, and its assertions and questions and commands. I don't want words, I need God!' And the idea is given that words are offering to needy people a stone when what they are asking for is bread.

This is an unfortunate misunderstanding. Basically, it is not the words themselves that we are focusing on, like lexicographers or students of linguistics do, but what the words depict. For words have senses, and employed in sentences they can refer to the realities they pick out. If you ask me where the milk is and I reply 'It is in the fridge,' you don't then proceed to open a word 'fridge' and drink the word 'milk.' Quite the opposite. The words facilitate you going to the fridge, opening it, and getting the milk. Likewise when one believes that Jesus Christ came into the world to save sinners, the focus is not exclusively on the words. Rather, since the words are not just about Jesus but are true of him, they have a kind of transparency. To trust the words about Jesus is to trust Jesus because Jesus is made known through the words.

And though Scripture does not present itself like a paper on nuclear physics or a piece of philosophical reasoning, its readers must use their reason to receive its message. As we saw earlier when Luke points to Paul's 'true and rational words' with which he spoke to Festus and Agrippa in Acts 26.25, he is referring to matters which were intelligible and verifiable and which they had heard. The Bible has to be interpreted by the use of our own resources, and with the assurance of the Lord's help when we do so.

We must try to read the Bible with correct expectations. Scripture is not an encyclopaedia, nor a book of science, nor a cookery book, nor a commentary on ancient politics. If we are tempted to think it is, then we shall come to the Bible with the wrong sort of outlook, expecting things that we will not find. We shall wander, looking for the wrong things, to the neglect of the main plot or narrative. The Bible is focused, and so there are matters which it does not mention or handle, or only touches on. We must not be tempted to twist it into something it was never intended to be.

A PARADOX

So there is a kind of paradox here. The location of the action which the Bible records is very defined and particular. All that it has to say took place in the Middle East, most of it in Palestine and the ancient Mediterranean world. Most of the participants were Jewish. But its message is not confined to these places.

Just as what happened at Runnymede had a definite location (in the Thames basin) and time in the year 1215, nevertheless through the Magna Carta it had an impact which resounds down the centuries and it had an international significance. So it is with the Bible, but in a much greater way. Its particular narrative has a universal importance, that transcends the Middle East but never leaves it behind because of what happened there. The great impact of the message of Scripture is part of the story: we have already noted Jesus' Great Commission, his charge to make disciples of all nations, teaching them about his own authority and being assured of his presence through the ministry of the Holy Spirit accompanying his disciples wherever he might lead them.

The Bible is set out in roughly historical sequence, which is part of its character. One thing leads to another, so that in the reading of the Bible the earlier is to be taken account of in the later writings. That is not to say that the Bible is nothing but history: it includes supernatural intrusions and has an overriding supernatural purpose. By and large it uses words not specially defined for their place in it, or specially tuned, but as they are use in the surrounding culture. As well as recording divine actions, the purpose of history within Scripture is to record the failings and successes of the people of God and their enemies, and how they respond or fail to respond to the Word of God. So we must have a very good reason to take the Bible out of sequence. To try to place ourselves into the history, for example, is a weird undertaking.

The New England pastor and theologian Jonathan Edwards (1703-1758) records the example of a man seeking guidance from the Bible as to whether or not he should go abroad. Suppose that after praying, the following verse (from Genesis 46:3) should 'suddenly and extraordinarily' come into his mind: 'fear not to go down into Egypt... and I will go with thee; and I will surely bring thee up again,' and is taken as God's direction for his life. The original meaning of the verse refers to Jacob; the man gives it another meaning. Edwards comments that to understand the Scripture 'is rightly to understand what is in the Scripture, and what was in it before it was understood... and not the making of a new meaning.'

LOOKING BACK AND THEN FORWARD

In this chapter we have taken up the question of what to expect when we pick up the Bible to read it seriously. It is a set of human documents, but it is also God's Book, the God who comes down to us, taking on our nature. It is not a magic book. We have to recognize this, and not take the books of the Bible to be what they are not. An email from Jack is not to be taken as one from Jill.

What is true of the Bible as a whole is true of the coming of Jesus Christ, the climactic figure in the entire Scriptural narrative. He does not arrive in pomp and political power. He was born in a stable. His parents had to escape into Egypt to prevent him being slaughtered by Herod. In his adult life he had no place to lay down. He had to deal with his disciples' crazy ideas: they repeatedly thought that he was trying to lead a revolt against the Romans. Yet John says of the Incarnate God, 'we have seen his glory, glory as of the only Son from the Father, full of grace and truth' (John 1.14). What did John and the believing remnant in his day see?

Clearly, discipline and empathy are required, and (above all) the guidance of God the Holy Spirit, if we are to follow John and the others. It is through such effort that we shall be able to discern its purpose as the unique sort of book it is. Acquiring such discernment is a lifelong business. In that way we shall better see the character of the God who has inspired its human words, and has acted wonderfully. We shall be aware of something of the glory of God in the face of Jesus Christ, who is the climax of the narrative, the point of it all. Above all, we need the opening of our hearts that only the Holy Spirit can make happen.

NEXT

Based on what we have begun to learn we shall begin to consider the character of that authority and how it is exercised. We began with the idea of an arrow, pointing downwards. Scripture records God's coming down. God comes to us, we are not to develop our own ideas. God is God, whether we approve of him or not. This is the dominant motif of the Bible. We have tried to sketch the character of this condescension. The Bible, a book inspired by him is his vehicle to us. In the next chapter we shall consider the authority of the Bible. Now we must think of the arrow reaching our hearts as we take in what the Bible teaches, and then changing our life's direction as we begin to respond. How is the Bible to exert its authority over us? What is our response to be?

2. THE BIBLE'S AUTHORITY

The first chapter claimed that central to engaging mind and heart with Scripture is coming to an appreciation of what kind of book it is and the need to discipline our thinking in the light of its character. Scripture's central claim that it is the word of God is all of a piece with the glory of the Incarnate Christ, that of glory in suffering. God reveals himself uniquely, but partially and obliquely, in his Son, a person who was misunderstood from the first by his those he came to, but whose birth was recognized by a faithful remnant as the birth of a king. The Author of life was denied and murdered, but God raised him from the dead (Acts 3:15). If he is the Son of God, one God with the Father, and imbued with the life of the Holy Spirit, and if the Bible is God's word, then we have a solemn responsibility to consider his claims carefully and prayerfully.

If the Bible is God's word, then it has authority. Yet

'authority' can come in various forms. We distinguish between authority that is given (such as that of MPs voting in the House of Commons) and authority that is earned by dint of genius and hard work. The MPs have delegated authority, that of Einstein is earned. And there are other kinds of authority. Parental authority is acquired, and conditional on its more or less efficient exercise. This conditional kind of authority can be removed or lessened by the activity of the state. Authority often has this character, that of teachers and doctors, for example.

In our day it is fair to say that the idea of authority has suffered something of an eclipse. In the West we are suspicious of all authority, except that which is conferred by 'democracy', or eyewitness authority, and perhaps that of an expert professional. Even these are increasingly viewed with scepticism. This attitude is an obstacle to understanding and coming to terms with divine authority.

The authority of Scripture is rather different from such authority, of course. In claiming to be God's word it implies that its authority is from God. If a person comes to recognize that authority, it follows that he ought to accept it. For God is the living God, our Creator and Lord, the sum of all perfection. He has authority because we owe everything to him, and because of his perfect character, which cannot be trumped by any other authority. Under certain conditions we ought to obey God and not obey the laws enacted in Parliament, or the commands of our parents or of experts. Their authority is conditional, but God's authority cannot be subordinate to some higher authority, for who or what could that be?

Nevertheless this is the authority of the God who stoops. Jesus spoke with authority, and not as the scribes. Never a man spoke like this man. But there is a warning on this packet. It is a divisive authority. When the Pharisees recognized what Jesus was claiming they took steps to kill him.

A PUBLIC DOCUMENT

So how do we go about coming to discover or to conclude that the Bible is what it claims to be? One of the matters we noted in the first chapter is that the Bible is a book, a public document. And further to that, it is about events in the public world. It is not simply a book about a person's stream of consciousness consisting of meditations, though it does have strands of such meditations, in the Psalms for example. It is a publicly available account about mostly public events, situated in the past, in the world of space and time. Furthermore we saw that some of these events are a crucial and pivotal part of Scripture, and so a crucial and pivotal part of human life. As far as the reading of Scripture is concerned these events are primary and essential to making any sense of the rest. In one place Paul wrote that if Christ has not been raised from the dead, his preaching is vain and faith in Christ would be pointless. We would still be in our sins (1 Corinthians 15:14).

The Bible does not take us to an imaginary country, as the writings of J.K. Rowling or J.R.R. Tolkien do, but to the Middle East, to Palestine and Egypt and Syria and Turkey, to events occurring two thousand years ago and more before our own time. So a preliminary way the Bible may be validated is by seeing if it fits into history. Was there a Jericho or Jerusalem? A Sea of Galilee? A River Euphrates? A road to Damascus from Jerusalem and so on and on? And a question of a rather different kind: were there miracles, or likely to have been?

What we are doing in trying to answer these questions involves basic answers about history and geography and culture, and sometimes more complex questions, about particular events in an area at certain times in the past. We could in this way build up a picture of the reliability of the documents of the Bible, at least those that are historical. Certain narratives fall outside this, due to their genre. For example we cannot expect to have historical or geographical corroboration of events in Jesus' parables, or the apocalyptic scenes in parts of Ezekiel or Daniel or Revelation. These are not themselves intended to be historical.

This reminds us that we must have regard to what the writers of the books of the Bible are intending. If there are places in which they are not intending to record real events then we should not expect to find traces of these events, or corroborations of them from other sources.

Such a historical approach to the claimed events in Scripture is not to be spurned as a way of trusting it. But it only takes the reader so far. Crucially, it would not stretch to the conclusion that the Bible, securely situated though it may be in the Middle East long ago, is God's word. It would have historical authority to varying degrees, even to a high degree in many cases, though its conclusions would always be subject to correction and confirmation. When I say 'to a high degree' I mean that the manuscript evidence for the Bible is vastly superior to that of, say, the ancient historians Herodotus and Thuycidides, or of the writings of Plato or Aristotle, which are taken for granted. Such an emphasis might be sufficient to get some people to take the Bible seriously. But it does not follow from such reliability that the Bible is God's word. Perhaps we could trust a person or group to verify the Bible for us. But that seems to be more of the same. Somehow, we need to have evidence of a different order than historical evidence. What kind of evidence could that be?

In skeptical and indifferent times, the efforts of scholars to show that the Bible fits snugly into what is known about the ancient Near East has value. The world is filled with every sort of cranky religious and spiritual scheme and so it is valuable to have this historical work. Archaeology, and the history of manuscripts, and written

ancient history are all of value. The writers of the Old
Testament as of the New take pains with the setting of
what they write (e.g Jeremiah 1, Acts 1).

A word of caution is needed, nevertheless. Efforts to
make the inspiration and authority of the Bible
'reasonable' can backfire. The Bible does not present
itself as being 'reasonable' in many of the connotations
that this slippery word has. It is not 'reasonable' in the
sense that the reasonable man easily and normally assents
to it. It has a mysterious side even as it has an accessible
side. In one of what seem to have been early Christian
'forms of words' that encapsulate the faith, it is stated
that 'Great indeed, we confess, is the mystery of
godliness':

> He was manifested in the flesh,
> vindicated by the Spirit,
> seen by angels,
> proclaimed among the nations,
> believed on in the world,
> taken up in glory.

— 1 TIMOTHY 3:16

This mini-confession is almost wholly taken up with
the mysterious side of the faith, that which seems to
beyond the probing powers of historians of the Near East.

When Paul discusses and defends the resurrection of

Christ, he begins by setting out at length some of the verifiable historical side of Jesus' resurrection, citing some of those who saw the risen Jesus. But the clinching argument for the resurrection is none of this data, but rather that had Jesus not been raised then Paul's preaching and faith in Jesus would have been in vain. The inner logic of the faith demands that Jesus be raised, as he himself said 'Was it not necessary that the Christ should suffer these things and enter into his glory' (Luke 24:26)?

So historical corroboration can only take us so far. We need to see why.

DIFFERENT SITUATIONS

To show this, let us begin by taking some steps back. Does a person have to believe that the Bible is the word of God to be a Christian? I answer, certainly not! If believing the Bible to be the word of God were necessary for that, then no one could have trusted Christ until there were was a completed Bible. And the Bible could not therefore have recorded men and women becoming Christians. But it does record many accounts of people coming to Christ: the thief on the cross, for instance, the disciples of Christ, the eunuch who was a courtier of Candace queen of Ethiopia (Luke does not tell us his name, Acts 8:26f), though he had a part of what became the Bible, Lydia the seller of purple was in a similar position (Acts 16:14), and so on. Churches of believers were formed in Jerusalem, Rome, Corinth, Ephesus and many other places, before the Bible was completed. And what about Abraham and all who followed in his steps, men and women of faith in God's promises? Think of that great roll-call of the faithful recorded in Hebrew 11.

So what is going on? Well, in the first place these facts show us that the circumstances of people vary. Some had only the Old Testament; Gentiles, who believed Paul, such as the few who believed him when he preached at Athens, would initially have very little to go on. But, and this is what is vital, they had some of the word of God such as promises, or fragments of the apostolic witness, and so on. When Paul preached about the Resurrection and the Judgment, Damaris and Dionysius and some others received what Paul taught with faith (Acts 17:34). Others like Lydia, who met Paul and Luke and others on the riverside at Philippi and whose heart the Lord opened so that she gave attention to Paul's teaching, may already have had some knowledge of the Old Testament (Acts 16:14).

Different people, different situations. But all were united by the fact that they had some of the word of God, some of the awareness of the glory of God shining in the face of Jesus Christ, and were confronted by its claims upon them. And as a consequence of the Lord opening their hearts, in one way and another they trusted Paul (or whoever the teacher was) and through them trusted Jesus. They became believers, part of 'the Way.' They came one by one to discern that the words they heard were also God's words and met their deepest needs.

These events give us a pattern for thinking of the Bible as a whole. In the baldest terms, these people, in responding to the good news of Jesus Christ, came to trust in the promises of God. So the pattern is *trusting the promises of God*. The New Testament cites Abraham as the prototype of the believer. He believed God (Romans 4), but on the other hand there were those who *dismissed the promises of God*. And trusting the promises occurs as a consequence of human spiritual and moral need, and of the knowledge of the sufficiency of the glory Christ, and the glory of his self-giving loving service for the undeserving, the weary and heavy laden.

PARABLES

We have seen that the general authority of Scripture is oblique, like the parables of Jesus. By the general authority here I mean the tendency of the whole book, the sixty-six books. This tendency is not simply informative, though I hope it is clear that it does have that force. It tells us things about God and ourselves that we would not otherwise know. If we read the Bible we learn things, but it is not only informative. The parables of Jesus are not simply charming tales. They have a *sifting* character, Jesus tells his disciples. We'll take a moment or two to consider this.

After Jesus had told the parable of the sower, and his disciples and others had asked him about it, he spoke generally about why he told parables. It is rather surprising. He said that to his disciples 'has been given the secret of the kingdom of God, but for those outside everything is in parables.' He then notes a passage of the Old Testament: 'They may indeed see but not perceive, and may indeed hear but not understand, lest they should turn and be forgiven' (Mark 4:12). The words were from Deuteronomy 2. Telling parables was central to his ministry: 'He said nothing to them without a parable' (Matthew 13:34).

When we read the Bible we must expect to find some things that we don't want to believe. Here in teaching about the parables, Jesus distinguishes two sorts of reactions: *seeing* but *not perceiving*, and *hearing* but *not believing*. The Bible can be an awkward, unsettling book. This is the basic problem with it, not difficulties with the authenticity of its manuscripts or 'the issue of miracles', or even of its consistency. Its authority includes this awkwardness. The words of Jesus, for example, caused division, and he knew they would (Luke 12:51). So when it is suggested that the basic stance in receiving the Scripture is trusting the promises of God, it is important also to bear in mind this other side of things.

MORE ABOUT AUTHORITY

I said earlier that it is obvious that to come to faith in Jesus it is not necessary to have the entire Bible. And coming to accept its authority is not simply a matter of information. Here I want to stress another feature of the situation. There is not one and only one approved way of accepting the authority of Christ. A person may be born into a home in which the Bible is treated as God's book. Another may come from an altogether different background, not knowing much about Christianity except the distortions he learns from the media. He may be turned around by what someone tells him about Jesus or by a preacher, or by reading a bit of a book about Jesus, or getting into an argument with someone. The New Testament is striking about the seemingly casual way in which it discloses itself. We are all different. And certainly there is not one set of Four Easy Steps to coming to accept the authority of Scripture.

So what is this difference between seeing and perceiving, and hearing and understanding? This is what we shall explore a little further. When we see and do not perceive, we see what others see; there is no defect in our sight. The problem is that we fail to see the significance in what we see, while others do see that significance. This is a common situation in everyday life: standing on the river bank you see what I see, the water, the weed, the pebbles, the far bank. But I don't see the trout. I did not know what to look for, perhaps; how a trout looks in clear, running water. Receiving Christ and his teaching, the significance of it, is a bit like this. So Jesus referred to those who have ears to hear (Mark 11:15). And he gave the fact that some failed to hear as the reason why they did not come to him. Sometimes it was not like the trout but because of moral barriers. Jesus said to some Pharisees, 'How can you receive me when you are busy with giving and receiving honours from one another?' We don't find this sort of issue in a book on engineering design, or the newspaper, or even a novel. It is part of the character of the authority of the Bible that its teaching needs to have the right reception.

So coming to faith in Christ is distinct from recognizing the authority of Scripture, though it is like it. Faith in Christ's authority and in Scripture's authority are distinct but overlapping, continuous. After all, the Bible could not exercise its authority until there is a Bible and until it was translated into your language. The assembling of the Bible was a lengthy and somewhat unclear business. More on that later.

THE GLORY OF GOD

When the apostle John was writing about the coming of Jesus he said that Jesus was the Logos, the eternal Word of God, and that he came, incarnate, to men and women. 'And the Word became flesh and dwelt among us, and we have seen his glory, glory as of the only Son from the Father, full of grace and truth' (John 1:14). This was the revelation of the glory of God in the face of Jesus Christ. But, remembering what we were saying earlier, this was not the outward display that we are accustomed to think of as glory. Paul made the contrast between the two sorts of glory explicit when he wrote of the 'secret and hidden wisdom of God,' and goes on: 'none of the rulers of this age understood this, for if they had, they would not have crucified the Lord of glory' (1 Corinthians 2:8).[1] The contrast is clear. The revealed glory of God in Jesus is one thing; it can be perceived but not seen. Worldly glory is another.

We must take this a stage further, to take in another aspect. In his second letter to the Corinthians Paul continues this theme of the character and location of true wisdom and power. He is concerned that the public ministry of the church should be consistent with this. And it should not be delivered in an underhand or cunning way, or involve tampering with God's truth in any way (2 Corinthians 4). He goes on:

> For what we proclaim is not ourselves, but Jesus Christ as Lord, with ourselves as your servants for Jesus' sake. For God, who said, 'Let light shine out of darkness,' has shone in our hearts to give the light of the knowledge of the glory of God in the face of Jesus Christ.

Once more we see that *matter* and *manner* are closely linked. If the gospel is about the glory of God revealed in Jesus, how he came, what he taught and what he suffered, then how the gospel is presented must be consistent with that. But Paul goes further. He quotes from the account of the creation in Genesis 1 and then shows that the light of God in the hearts of men and women is to give them the knowledge of Jesus' true glory. Those who see the true glory of God in Jesus do so as a result of the personal enlightening of God.

So there are two sides to God's activity. There is the public objective ministry of Jesus, and what he suffered, and the preaching of this by apostles and ministers, reflecting the public character of the Scripture. And there is an inner work of God's Spirit of opening the inner eyes of men and women, turning seeing into perceiving. There is the authority of God in his message, his word, and there is inner recognition of this authority. Notice too how strong Paul's words are: the result of this inner working is like light shining in darkness.

What I have been trying to do is to show that the factors at work in receiving the inspiration and authority of Scripture are of a piece. There is the outward factor of God's word inspired and the inner factor of God making the content of this word apparent to men and women.

Each, inspiration and regeneration, is the special work of
God the Holy Spirit.

SELF-AUTHENTICATION AND SCRIPTURE

So an important, decisive feature of the word of God
generally, and the gospel in particular, is that it 'speaks for
itself.' Let us think again of Abraham, the father of the
faithful. When the Lord appeared to him, and promised
him that his offspring would be innumerable and he
believed the Lord (Genesis 15:6), was this a leap of faith?
Was he taking a big risk? The Bible does not suggest that
he was. His reliance was due to is God-given
understanding, upon God's self-presentation. He took the
Lord at his word and he believed God.

I hope it is clear from our discussion so far that a
person can recognize the self-evident character of the
gospel to him or her without reading a Bible. For as
noted, in the paradigmatic case of faith, Abraham
receiving the covenant promises of God, believing God,
was in the early days of the Lord's revealing himself.
There was as yet no New or Old Testament.

This, the subjective side to inspiration, recognizing
the divine authority of Scripture, has to do with its
matter, with what it asserts. It is important that this self-
authentication involves a kind of recognition. It is *not* new
evidence. It is not a voice whispering 'This is the inspired
word of God, one of 66 books...' For one thing, relying on

such a voice would simply put recognition back one stage. For how would we recognise the authenticity of the voice? Relying on such a voice would be what used to be called 'enthusiasm,' the founding of religion not on the objective voice of God in Scripture, but on a new revelation, a new voice, to me.

To understand what such basic recognition involves we must see that because of our fallen-ness there are barriers to recognition that arise from our sinful nature. There is mist, a distortion, a disaffection. In our heart of hearts we do not want to receive what God reveals. We have put the shutters up, indeed the entire human race is shuttered up. The many 'explanations' of the Christian religion in political or social or psychological terms are ways of voicing this disaffection. So we need enlightening. Of course we may need information too, because we have not appreciated some fact or feature of the revelation. But it's not so much that we need education as appreciation. We need to see the facts as they are, to appreciate their importance and significance. We need sensitizing.

How do we obtain this? It is a gift that is beyond price. To see this, let us reflect on Paul's expressions to the Corinthians again. He speaks of 'enlightenment,' the shining of God into our hearts. For Paul and the Corinthians to whom he is writing, God has shined into their hearts to give them the knowledge of God in (reflected in) the face of Jesus Christ. This is the work of

God's Spirit, the Holy Spirit (if you study what Paul wrote it clearly involves the activity of the entire Trinity). Once we see this, as we get the idea, the need for and the gift of such recognition springs up all over the New Testament. For example, in events recorded. When some people abandoned Jesus, he asked the twelve, 'Do you want to go away as well?' Peter said (speaking for them all, as seems to have been usual), 'Lord, to whom shall we go? You have the words of eternal life, and we have believed and have come to know that you are the Holy One of God' (John 6:67f). And in Jesus' teaching, again to Peter, after his confession that Jesus was the Christ, the Lord's anointed, Jesus responded 'Blessed are you, Simon Bar-Jonah! For flesh and blood has not revealed this to you, but my Father who is heaven' (Matthew 16:15f.). This might be paraphrased, 'you have come to this conclusion not as a result of sensory perception, but with a recognition granted by God himself.'

This is not the place to go into detail of this ready response of faith in Christ, but we need to say a word or two more. It is a mixed response, in the sense that it has this positive side and a negative side. It is faith, the positive side, that arises out of conviction and sin and penitence, the negative side. People such as Peter are cases of the 'weary and heavy laden' to whom Jesus gives rest. There are other examples of these in the Gospels and in the Acts of the Apostles. Part of the glory of God's revelation is that it provides many accounts of men and women receiving the Saviour. It follows the pattern of 'faith comes from hearing, and hearing through the word of Christ' (Rom. 10. 17). Those who come to Christ need to know about him, obviously, but they need to have their eyes opened like Peter and the others. And it is also a partial response, in the sense that there is always more of the word of God to understand and appreciate that strengthens our faith and that guides and prompts the life of discipleship that follows.

So, before we change gear, we note that we have seen in this section that the eyes of our hearts need to be opened to receive what God has done and will do for us (Ephesians 1:18). We credit God as being true to what he says. We recognise the glorious character of what he has said and done in coming down to us in Christ.

THE CANON

Now we return to the Bible as such. The New Testament as we have it is often referred to as part of the canon of Scripture, complementing and completing the canon of the Old Testament. That is, the books in these two canons together form the boundaries of God's special revelation, containing all things necessary for our salvation. So that when people referred to 'the inspiration of Scripture' this is what they are referring to. 'Canon' means 'rule.' So the canonical books together have this normative standing. They are the sacred deposit of his word.

Surprisingly, perhaps, there is a considerable measure of obscurity as to how the New Testament canon came to be. It was not through any formal church decision. The New Testament consists of four Gospels, the 'Acts of the Apostles' (which is clearly a continuation of the Gospel of Luke), a number of letters of Paul's, some of John, and Peter, one of James's and Jude's, and one (the Letter to the Hebrews) whose authorship is not clear. Finally there is the Revelation to John.

The Church affirmed that all the books in the New Testament canon are indeed God's word written, but the Church did not 'decide' which books are in the canon in a formal meeting. Rather the Church recognised the inherent inspiration of books in a reasonably halting and uneven way. The process was more 'bottom up' via local churches, than 'top down' from a big Church Council. The actual process, as best we can reconstruct it, was uneven and non-miraculous. Letters that were initially sent to individuals (e.g. 3 John) or were not associated with an apostle, took slightly longer to be widely recognised. By the time of Augustine (354-430), the 27 books of our New Testament were recognised (Augustine listed them) but he was aware that they were 'not received by all.' What came to be the full set of canonical writings, Old and New Testament, came to be united in one book. The criteria were like those we have noted: objectivity, that is, their apostolic provenance, and subjectivity, that they gave evidence of their God-givenness, person by person. In Justin's, (AD100-165) words, they were 'big with power.'

The Old Testament gives an account of the Creation and Fall, and then the Covenant with Abraham and with all that followed the establishment of the people of Israel, their presence in Egypt and deliverance from bondage, the entry into the land of promise, and the subsequent history of Israel. All this was framed by a series of divine covenants, and Messianic prophecies fulfilled by Jesus. His coming was the fulfilment of God's promise of a deliverer for the people of God, and he was recognized by a faithful remnant of believers in an Israel that was then under the occupation of the Romans.

After Jesus' death and resurrection, there was an expectation among the apostles and their circle that God who spoke in the Old Testament, would speak once more. The Holy Spirit, the Spirit of truth was their promised teacher (John 15:26). They read the words of Micah, 'For out of Zion shall go forth the law, and the word of the Lord from Jerusalem' (Micah 4:2), and remembered that their Lord to whom they bare witness 'in Jerusalem, and in all Samaria' (Luke 24:47; Acts 1:8) had promised that the Holy Spirit would come.

Note again the 'humanness' of this background of the formation of a canon. If this is the word of God then it was the result not of a heavenly divine proclamation, like the giving of the Ten Commandments (Exodus 20:18), but almost casually, certainly obscurely, by acts of divine providence. Initially, there seems to be a mismatch between what is claimed of them and how they actually emerged. What were the criteria that showed their authenticity? Obviously a strong connection with the ministries of the Apostles which was no doubt visible to begin with, but then was accepted as the churches would receive, by circulation, writings which were new to them. That connection was sometimes via authorship, as in Paul's and John's letters. Besides this, a historical connection with the apostles and their 'apostolicity', a word that covers both the provenance of the writings and their content, commended themselves. This process, it seems, is akin to that of self-authentication discussed earlier. After all, as we have been seeing, the New Testament contains not only what God said and did for us in Jesus, but also accounts of the ways in that this was received by the men and women, singly and in families, who came to be the early church, the followers of the Way.

Yet puzzles about the canon remain. Not everything the apostles wrote and circulated had canonical status. In Corinth, in the hall of Tyrannus, Paul reasoned for two years about the kingdom of God (Acts 19:9). But not a shred of this seems to have come down to us. In Paul's letter to the Colossians he advised that 'when this letter has been read among you, have it also read in the church of the Laodiceans; and see that you also read the letter from Laodicea' (Colossians 4:16). What was this letter from Laodicea? It is not in the New Testament. What happened to it? Maybe it refers to a letter of Paul's that had in its circulation reached the Laodiceans. In 1 Corinthians 5:9 Paul reminds his readers 'I wrote to you in the letter not to associate with the sexually immoral' and in 2 Corinthians 2:4 he refers to an earlier letter written with much affection and anguish of heart and with many tears.' What were these letters? 1 Corinthians does not seem to match this description. While puzzles remain in the mysterious business of the formation and recognition of the New Testament canon, on the biblical understanding of authority, scripture and faith outlined so far, these puzzles do not undermine scripture's authority.[2]

3. **OBJECTIVITY**

We have covered a good deal of ground already. This chapter is a sort of breathing space, as we shall here look in more detail at one or two issues identified and presupposed in our first two chapters. We have stressed that the Bible is a real object, containing sixty-six books, the canon of the Christian faith. But now I want to make and stress a further point, that the Bible possesses objectivity, and presents its message as not simply a set of opinions, but as the truth regarding people and God. Not only that, but these truths have a permanent value and importance. The inspiration of Scripture is epitomised in faith's trust in the sure promises of God. They are 'timelessly true' in a sense that we shall discuss later on.

Such a chapter as this may not have been necessary years ago. But nowadays it is important to insist on something that we cannot take for granted, that the account of the world around us (and within us) consists of objective truths. If something is true in this sense, it is true whether we like it or not. Our culture is at present strongly affected by skepticism, and one strong, fashionable cultural current in reaction to this is some kind of subjectivity or relativism. Put crudely, Jack can be heard to say 'Certain things are true for me and my group' and Jill says 'But different and contrary things are true for me and my group.' And this skeptical and relativistic mood can affect the Christian faith both in its presentation and also in its reception. More particularly for us, it can affect the way in which we understand the Bible.

Such moods and movements are often defended in the name of human freedom and creativity. They have a strong 'constructivist' strain, as we shall see. Of course much in our culture exists as a result of human beings creating things. Engineering, architecture, and what we generally refer to as 'technology' lead to productions which are often awe-inspiring. Mount Everest is not such an artefact, but the Tower of London and the Eiffel Tower are; and the development of atomic power and lunar missions most certainly are. They are examples of obvious and striking human constructs. Many are more mundane, but still are every bit as elaborate and sophisticated human creations. And the same goes for art and literature. More and more of our intellectual environment has this constructed character. In this chapter I want to discuss

this side of things, and how it affects our understanding of
the Word of God.

CONSTRUCTIVISM

Such constructs, both scientific and in the varied contents
of human minds, help to engender the idea of what I shall
call *constructivism*. The idea is that the human mind is free
to construct reality and indeed we are free to construct
our own identity as human beings. Modern electronics
has enabled us to build and to enjoy virtual realities,
realities which we can 'enter' at will. And prompted by
this and similar developments, such as mind-altering
drugs, some have gone so far as to blur the distinction
between fact and fiction. Even one's gender is capable of
re-construction, it is said. Religion is also affected by this
mood, this sort of creativity. So it becomes but a short
step for people to think of religion as nothing but the
product of human fancy and imagination. Is not the Bible
and what it teaches us only one example of many of such
creations?

The truth is that to blur what is objective with what is
subjective in this wholesale way, to talk seriously of a
plurality of realities and of constructing realities, is a case
of wild exaggeration. It cannot be carried through
consistently. Those who move in this direction are
indulging in a fashion that has not been thought through.
Those who fantasize and who hypothesize in this way

rapidly come up against a world that is altogether firmer and more resistant than the world of make-believe. They forget that though we can ignore history, what has happened is fact. We may for example try to deny that there was such a person as Oliver Cromwell, or despise or dislike him, but we cannot wish him away and create a reality in which he has not existed. That cannot be altered. Reality is not pliable in a way that such creativity unthinkingly assumes. It has sharp edges. Putting things more formally, it is impossible to hold this constructivist position consistently. Reality, real reality, keeps upsetting things.

However energetic the efforts to construct the world may be, the real world of space and time asserts itself. I may make up for myself a new identity in a brave new world that I have devised, but the real world makes itself evident before I get very far. This shows itself in the satisfaction of realities such as the need to sleep and to eat. I cannot wish away the objectivity of middle-sized material objects. I lean on the table and strike my shin on the chair. I am reminded that my salary has not been paid in this month and that gas bill needs paying. I am affected by alcohol or sunshine, and there is the fact that I grow older and grow tired, whether I like it or not. Other people make demands on me. And there is the inescapable destiny of my dying and death. I may believe that my entire life is a dream, but reality will keep making itself manifest. Yes, there is human construction—history and culture is full of it. But the deeper, story-book fantasy, alternative reality, is a parasite on the hard and firm reality of the world in which we live.

Of course we all make mistakes in our perceiving and thinking: mistaking what day of the week it is, or whether the lampshade is really white, or whether the man who introduced himself to me was called 'Dave' and even whether there was a piano against the wall. Our senses may become worn out in later years and in any case may play tricks on us. But the point is that there are established ways of checking myself: by consulting a calendar, or checking colour against a chart, or asking what others see, or comparing my sense of sight with other senses, or vice versa.

THE SUBJECTIVITY OF THE POINT OF VIEW?

This and what follows reminds us of what we have already discussed, that the Scriptures and what they report as history take their place in this objective world. The Christian does not make room for himself and his religion by subjectivizing the Bible. The history presented in the Bible is embedded in human history more generally.

But isn't the view that Jesus Christ came into the world to save sinners simply a point of view, even (some might say) a leftover from the Victorians? This question and questions like it are perhaps much more prevalent than the deeper fantasizing that people indulge in what we have been discussing and they are more worrying. 'You have your opinion and I have mine.' A Christian may see in such language the working of a mechanism that is designed to put a distance between the speaker and the claims of Scripture. So let us think a little more carefully about it.

FREEDOM TO THINK

It is a consequence of living in a country in which people have freedom of speech that a person has the right to his point of view, however bizarre. But it does not follow from this sociological fact that every point of view is as worthwhile as any other.

A more subtle attenuation of objectivity occurs in an attitude to ancient writings which begins with the claim that every such writing must be understood in terms of its own context, meaning the historical and cultural setting in which it is produced. As it stands this remark is innocuous, even helpful. After all, who wants to do violence to a writing by assuming that it has no context, or by assuming it is a fake written in the last decade? Respecting the context means taking account of the style and vocabulary of the author's language, the writer's outlook, what he knew and was ignorant of, the intended readership of the writing, and so on. There are recognized ways in which today's reader of ancient writings goes about this, finding out more and more about life in the remote past.

Take translation, for instance. No translation can perfectly replicate the original. But by successive efforts at understanding a text, including each nuance, the reader is able to get increasingly nearer to the meaning of the original. This involves attention to the original languages and the efforts needed of making sense of the writing in its original setting.

Sometimes the word 'context' is used in a sense in which it is held that appreciation of the context helps to form a protective wrapping that prevents access to what occurred at a particular time or place. The ancient writing is then treated like an exhibit in a glass case. We might reasonably ask the question of whether our interpretation and understanding of, for example, Augustine's writings are affected by the priorities of our own culture. But it is an exaggeration to suppose that each of us is cocooned within our own culture and that Augustine's writings are thus inaccessible. When Augustine's Latin is translatable into contemporary English, is something lost in that process? Obviously so. The original is not the translation. The contents of the mind of the author are not available to us and we cannot now or ever *be* Augustine. But then his mother Monica could not have had the mind of her brilliant son either. None of us can gain direct access into the mind of another, whether a contemporary or someone in the past (Proverbs 14:10). To have such direct access we would have to be that person, an impossibility. But just as we can understand a person better by listening to him and asking him questions, talking to his friends, and finding out how he spends his time, so a person may interrogate an ancient author and become immersed in his writings and outlook.

There is another matter. Past cultures and situations may themselves stand in need of critique. We should not allow sociology to blunt our faculties. What is, is not the same thing as what ought to be. Some contexts and cultures are supportive of the Christian faith, others oppose it. So we need to ask, in the case of some interpretation of the New Testament, is it selective and biased, neglecting some features because they do not accord with our contemporary agenda? Are we ourselves blinded in some such way?

There are moral values set forth in Scripture, which have been lost to our contemporary culture, or which as a matter of fact our culture hasn't sufficiently recognized. The Christian faith may judge the morals of our culture. It may be said that Paul's 'context' was different from that of the Corinthians to whom he wrote. He had certain beliefs and priorities and his readers may have had different beliefs and priorities. But Paul did not scruple to caution them regarding their beliefs (about the resurrection of the dead, for example) and their behavior (in regard to the relations between the sexes, or of the young to the old), by what he calls 'my gospel'.

A follower of Jesus or Paul must first apply their teaching to themselves before trying to do the same with others. But Paul has set a precedent and a pattern of assessing the contemporary culture by the gospel. Is this an easy task to undertake? No, most certainly not. There are numerous pitfalls. Is it impossible? No, most certainly not. For otherwise the church automatically accepts the culture, and the Bible's teaching is swamped, and what we are left with at best becomes a plaything of that culture.

THE PAST AND OURSELVES

In the case of interpreting the New Testament, in religion we must give it priority over the contemporary. Most people will find that attitude extraordinary, so convinced have we become that the latest is the best. Nevertheless, the Christian position is that the past must be allowed to exercise authority over the present. This goes against much of our modern Western culture, in which the contemporary is automatically regarded as superior in every respect to the past. The past is regarded as 'primitive', more gullible, and superstitious than our present sophistication. But in the Christian way of thinking, what occurred in the past must exercise authority over the present.

Not in every respect, of course. Nor is this a matter simply of keeping an open mind on the question of what the past might have to teach us, or of cultivating and maintaining an interest in history. It is more principled than that. In respect of our relationship to God the past is certainly essential because God's revelation, which is normative, was given in the past and culminated in the life, ministry, death and resurrection of the Incarnate Son of God. These were once-for-all events, and Christians live in the light of them because they provide a transforming outlook. This dependence on the past is not mere antiquarianism, but vital for a living church. Accepting this outlook is not to deny that that message must be presented in contemporary terms, though not in such a way as to undermine its timeless importance and international reach. We shall attempt to develop this point more fully in the next chapter.

So it is important that the channels between the past and the present are kept open, such that the objective character of what occurred in the history and religion depicted in the Bible are upheld and maintained. We must be on our guard of ways of thinking that are relative and subjective and which therefore clog up the channels.

MEANING AND ILLUMINATION

Earlier we stressed that the Christian faith at its heart has the idea of *trusting the promises of God*, and that the Bible's inspiration is an extension of these promises of God which are central to the piety of the people of God in the Old and New Testaments and subsequently. But what, more exactly, is the connection between faith on the one hand and that inspiration? Here is another context in which careful thinking is necessary in order to safeguard the objectivity of Scripture. The dangers of subjectivity are often close at hand, unfortunately.

Consider these words:

> To say 'the Word of God' is to say the Word of *God*. It is therefore to speak about a being and event which are not under control or foresight. Our knowledge of this being and event does not justify us in thinking and speaking of them as though they were under our control or foresight. We know this divine nature which we cannot control or foresee when we know this Word.

They are from Karl Barth, the influential twentieth-century theologian.[1] Note how this passage maintains that we know the Word of God only when God uses the words of Scripture, and Barth repeatedly stresses that the Word of God is not under our control or foresight. Rather the words of the Bible becoming the Word of God by divine activity is an act of divine freedom. Barth's point is that the Bible is not *permanently* the Word of God, but is on occasion activated by God's power and then lapses back into a collection of fallible ancient writings.

Earlier we stressed that the Bible is a book which has many of the features of any other book of ancient history.

And it is as such a book that it is God's revelation. Not that it becomes God's word for a time by a fresh act of God's freedom, but it is as it stands, that word. In this way God has accommodated himself, coming down to us. This word of God can be read and understood by anyone who is sufficiently interested, but in order to receive it as the Word of God something else is necessary: it needs the illumination of the Holy Spirit. God shines in our hearts, and the message of salvation that the Bible brings becomes personal to us. This is because readers may come to the Bible with various deep misconceptions. It is a book with a radical message of a personal kind. When we read it we are very likely to be put off by this personal impact, and immediately express our opposition using various strategies. When we read the text we may quickly conclude that it does not apply to ourselves. And so we distance ourselves from it. We may even see that it calls for serious changes in our lives and for that reason have nothing to do with it, like the Pharisees of Jesus's day (Matthew 21:25) or Paul's hearers at Athens (Acts 17:32).

What is happening when we do respond positively? It is not that besides the Bible there is an additional revelation. The Bible *is* God's revelation. Rather we are brought by the Spirit to see some of its implications, and particularly its personal implications. This may happen while there are still many things that we read in the Bible that puzzle us. If this is so then the best policy is to put such parts of the Bible 'on hold.' This is sometimes called implicit faith. We continue to believe things that at present we don't understand. Just as Jesus' disciples often misunderstood and mistook aspects of his teaching and sometimes tried to correct him, so there are always things in the Bible that we may not understand and even be exasperated with or annoyed about. The best policy is prayerful patience. We do not see what they mean, or how they fit into its overall teaching. There will be more to be said about 'implicit faith' in the next chapter.

There is revelation, and there is personal illumination. There is Word *and* Spirit. By contrast, for Barth the revelation only occurs at a time of God's choosing. We cannot foresee or control by turning the pages of the Bible, by Bible study, or listening to preaching what that 'word' is. So I'm suggesting that language such as Barth uses runs together two important ideas, revelation and illumination, that we have been distinguishing and that if we merge these ideas we put the objectivity of the revelation in jeopardy. The Bible itself shows us that the one word of God may have contrary effects. As we have noted, Jesus' ministry often had a divisive effect. What Paul taught as the Apostle to the Gentiles had diverse reactions, as we are shown time and again in the Acts of the Apostles. Paul himself said that what he preached was 'to one (of those being saved) a fragrance from death to death, to the other (those perishing) a fragrance from life to life' (2 Corinthians 2:16). So the very same teaching, with the same meaning, had diverse and contrary responses. In the Old Testament similarly, the prophet Ezekiel is instructed to utter his prophecy 'whether they hear or refuse to hear' (Ezekiel 2:5, 3:11, 3:27). Similarly with Christ's 'he who has ears to ear, let him hear' (for example, Mark 4:9).

Even within Christendom there are attitudes which have the effect of blunting the objectivity of 'the faith.'

CONTROL, GOD'S FREEDOM

The freedom (or sovereignty) of God is not seen in making something that was not the word of God to be, on occasion, the word of God. Otherwise there could never be disagreement. It was seen in two ways, firstly in the bringing to pass those events in which he comes to the human race, lost and needy, with his own love and grace. This process involves the covenant of God and its development and culmination in the giving of his Son, meaning the coming, ministering, suffering, and death and resurrection of Jesus Christ. Secondly, the illuminating of men and women to see their need of what God has graciously done for humankind. This involves an objective revelation, and the personal appropriation of that by God's Spirit. The entire Trinity, Father, Son and Holy Spirit, is at work in these processes, as we have already seen.

Some are tempted to the other extreme. They think of the church primarily as the place where they can find

friendship and help, or as the place where they can recite
old, familiar words and be comforted by them, by
maintaining Christian traditions learned in their
childhood. They may think of the church as a place where
their children can be taught certain standards of
behaviour, or where money can be raised for charity.

None of these things is wrong. The church is to be
involved in all these things. Most of the New Testament
was written not for individuals but for churches and the
corporate aspect of the Christian life is vital. But the
balance which the Word of God can give the church must
not be ignored. The danger is that we shall see the church
primarily as a centre of spiritual help and no more. In
terms we have been using, the church is not to do only
with satisfying our subjective needs: to focus on these
activities first and last is to have a one-dimensional view
of the church as a society or club. It is to forget the
objective, foundational side of things.

The church is what she is by virtue of what she
believes. She is the body of Christ, a staggeringly strong
idea but one which is stressed in the New Testament.
This expression highlights the church's uniqueness. She is
what she is by virtue of who Jesus Christ is and what he
has done for the people who form the church. That is, her
identity is in virtue of the objective facts about Jesus to be
found in Scripture. So, she is 'built on the foundation of
the apostles and prophets, Christ Jesus himself being the
cornerstone, whom the whole structure, being joined

together, grows into a holy temple in the Lord' (Ephesians 2:20-21). Where is that foundation located? The answer is that the foundation is in the words of divine revelation. Remember the opening words of the Letter to the Hebrews, words that overlap those just quoted. 'Long ago, at many times and in many ways, God spoke to our fathers by his prophets, but in these last days he has spoken to us by his Son...' (Hebrews 1:1).

So the church has a confessional basis. Creeds are recited and confessions subscribed to, not to pay honour to the church's founder in some vague way, but to actively testify to this unique foundation and, in consequence, to the unique role that she has in society. The language of the church is not some 'language game,' a private esoteric language of her own, heard only within her four walls. Rather, God has come down in Jesus, and the church responds by confessing her faith in daily life in thanksgiving and praise for her Saviour and Lord, and in obedience to him. The church is comprised of such people.

THE WORD AND THE CHURCH

In talking of the church as we have it may seem that we have strayed from our main business, God's revelation. Not a bit of it! The church, the assembly of the people of God, is the child of that revelation. Not a cosy cult, with a language of her own. Not an introverted social club. Not people who make a success of life, but the weary and heavy laden and the broken hearted who have found salvation and hope in what Christ has done. So the objectivity of that revelation, which we have been stressing against the various forces of subjectivism and relativism of today's culture, should find an echo in the objective foundation of the life of the church and of her impact in society.

We now return to consider further vital features of God's word.

In Chapter 2 I argued that the heart of the divine inspiration of Scripture is a mysterious two-author view of its production according to which the text is a result of the writing of Peter or Paul or Hosea or Jeremiah, reflecting the personality of each, and at the same the work of God's inbreathing.

The model of such inbreathing is the prophet or apostle, as seen for example in the book of Isaiah and the Letter to the Romans. The case of a Gospel or a book of Israelite history such as 1 Chronicles is what I call a compilation. The operation is rather different in such cases, in which the finished document consists of material that already existed, perhaps orally or in a writing, and is brought together by the compiler and made into a continuous narrative or a text of distinct episodes. The result is the equation, what Scripture says, God says, since God's in-breathing in the case of a prophecy, or his superintendence of the compilation, ensure that it is the speech of God as well as the writing or compilation merely of human beings. Of course the distinction between what is a compilation, and what is directly authored, is only one of degree. An author such as Paul has not made up his letters from scratch, in an absolute way. He partly uses what he himself will have been told or worked out, perhaps with the help of Luke during their journeys together or what is recorded in the Acts of the Apostles, using his judgment as to what he should include and what to leave out. In this he was divinely guided. Nonetheless he 'signs off' the resulting letter as his letter.

This reveals one important feature of Scripture, that it is a library of books having different genres or literary styles. In the Old Testament there is a book of poetry, the Psalms, as well as collections of sayings, the Book of Proverbs, and a book of stylized general personal reflections on human life, the book of Ecclesiastes. The New Testament consists of three stand-alone Gospels and Luke's two volumes of a Gospel and the Acts of the Apostles, apostolic letters to the churches and to certain individuals, and the Revelation, which is largely apocalyptic in character.

It is important to keep this variety in mind for at least two reasons. One we have already touched on, differences in the manner of authorship, and therefore in what we may call the 'inspiration process.' The other concerns the way we interpret or understand these books. Poetry is not prose, and a proverb is not an account of an event that has occurred in the past. And apocalyptic, in Ezekiel and Daniel or Revelation, is different again. Different and unfamiliar to a modern reader, certainly. When we take up one or other of the books of the Bible, we should do so with certain expectations that these different literary styles engender. And learning and becoming familiar with these expectations is part of what is involved in the exercise of reading the book, or perhaps a section of the book, when history suddenly changes to apocalyptic.

THE IDEA OF INFALLIBILITY

Recognizing these different literary styles in Scripture also has to do with our expectations about Scripture, its reach and character. We'll return to this after we have thought a little about the idea of infallibility.

Suppose that there is a person who unfailingly remembers and delivers the dates of the reigns of the Kings and Queens of England. We might say that in this regard, in the accurate answer to questions about the reigns, he is infallible. It is impossible to make him fail over the dates. He has a particular ability. At least, he possesses infallibility in some particular area. Or maybe a young person can unfailingly recite the ten times table. When she grows older, and becomes more forgetful, then maybe she will fail. But at present she is infallible on the times table.

Here we have some simple cases of how the possession of hum-drum, everyday infallibility may be acquired and displayed. But it is a weak sense, because the person may lose the ability, in a reverse process of acquiring it. And it is an infallibility that is confined to some particular area or subject of interest, and gained by the application of someone to acquiring a proficiency. And in a related way, there may be written infallibility. An almanac may contain a wholly reliable account of the year's tide-times for a series of coastal locations.

When we think of divine infallibility, we are thinking of a much stronger notion. What God can do, such as know all the stars, counting them, and naming them (Psalm 147:4) is not an acquired skill. He does not learn it, nor could he forget it. And it is a part of total infallibility, covering both the grandest and most minute features of the universe. It is a consequence of God's knowledge and power. In Psalm 139, David celebrates the range of God's knowledge. For example God discerns what David knows, he is acquainted with all his ways, even before his words reach the tip of his tongue, he knows what he is about to say. No wonder David exclaims 'Such knowledge is too wonderful for me; it is high; I cannot attain it' (Psalm 139:6). Here he introduces the idea of the incomprehensibility of God. His powers are so awe-inspiring because we cannot get our finite, space-bound and time-bound, minds around them. God's unfailing power is a product of his perfections. His knowing and willing are unfailing, necessarily unfailing, eternally unfailing. These divine powers are the basis of the bringing about of a distinct product such as the Bible, which has this divine property of being unfailing as a consequence of being the Word of God.

> When God desired to show more convincingly to the heirs of the promise the unchangeable character of his purpose, he guaranteed it with an oath, so that by two unchangeable things [the promise, and then the oath], in which it is impossible for God to lie, we who have fled for refuge might have strong encouragement to hold fast to the hope set before us.
>
> — HEBREWS 6:17,18

We are reminded again of the centrality of the promises of God in Scripture. Here is a promise with a double lock, the promise itself, and an oath. A promise worthy of the firmest trust. This example is particularly notable for us because it concerns God's *word*. His word of promise is worthy of our unconditional reliance. Divine promises have been fulfilled, the fulfilment of some of them is still future. The word of a liar provides no assurance; the word of the unfailing God is utterly trustworthy. As the writer of Hebrews tells us, it is founded on the greatness, the perfection of God, his unchangeableness.

Paying attention to the varied styles of the books of Scripture means also that we note what styles are missing from the Bible. For example, it does not contain any scientific papers, or handbooks for domestic appliances. No instructions for assembling flatpack furniture. No maps, or travel directions. There are guarantees, as we have seen, but no guarantees about the performance of a radio or phone. This is not simply because the Bible is a product of eras that are past, eras that we too-readily label 'primitive'. The absence of certain kinds of writings, and the confining of the writings to certain 'times' should alert us to what sort of a compilation of books the Bible is. All these remarks about the make-up of the Bible should help us to adjust our expectations when we read it.

INFALLIBILITY AND LITERARY STYLE

In thinking through what infallibility means as far as the Bible is concerned we need once again to relate it to its varied style, what the Bible does not contain as well as what it does. We need to bear these styles in mind, together with the related matter of the context in which the words and sentences and longer passages are found. Above all we need to bear in mind the overall purpose of the Bible, its scope, which as the Westminster Confession put it in 1646, is 'to give all the glory to God.' (I.5).

We need above all things to bear in mind what was earlier said about God coming down to us. The Bible is the literary deposit of that coming down, its history of the Lord's choice of a people to be the vehicle of the climax of his covenant, the appearing of Jesus Christ, the Messiah, the world's Saviour from sin, and the agent of the reconciliation of people from every corner of the globe to their God and Lord. As part of this, God has in his wisdom and goodness seen fit to provide this infallible document, his selective account of what he has done for us, so that we may ourselves come to Christ and enjoy his benefits now and in the world to come, which it also assures us of.

So another feature which we must bear in mind in reading the Bible, is that it is an incomplete account of God's purposes of redemption, in the sense that it leaves important threads dangling. It is very selective. It is written on a need-to-know basis. It is not an encyclopedia or even a text-book. There are important questions that it does not aim to answer. At the end of his Gospel, John puts this point in a striking way:

Now Jesus did many other signs in the presence of his disciples, which are not written in this book, but these are written, so that you may believe that Jesus is the Christ [that is, is God's anointed Messiah] the son of God, and that by believing you may have life in his name.

— JOHN 20:30; SEE ALSO JOHN 21:25

Reading the Bible may arouse our curiosity, and we may wonder about this and that feature of it, what is included and what is excluded, as well as wondering about what is hard to understand. It is worth remembering when this happens and queries and questions arise in our minds, that what we have is only part of the story. There is more to come. Jesus himself told his disciples that he had many things to tell them but that they could not bear them at that time. But he added that they would learn these things 'when the Spirit of truth comes', that his Holy Spirit, when Jesus had risen and ascended to his Father, and 'he will guide you into all truth' and 'will declare to you the things that are to come. He will glorify me, for he will take what is mine and declare it to you' (John 12:2f). No doubt this was a reference to the apostolic writings which complete the New Testament. And the same is true of our present situation. The Bible is not to be added to, but nevertheless we live, as pilgrim people, in the time between the work of Christ and the consummation of all things. We have 'a kingdom that cannot be shaken' (Hebrews 12:28).

So our understanding of Scripture must take into account its infallibility, but also the character of the writings that are infallible, and our present situation as it relates to the ongoing purposes of God. If there are certain outworkings of these purposes which we don't know, then this requires the development of a certain characteristic, patience, in our reading of the Bible. As we saw with matters that have been revealed in Scripture that we cannot immediately understand, we must be patient; not passive, but resolutely enduring.

The first disciples of Christ were in this position, and from what we learn in the gospels this was not an easy thing for them to come to terms with. Sometimes Christ had to rebuke them for their clumsiness and slowness. It would not be surprising if we, living further on, exhibited similar reactions.

SOME EXAMPLES

We are learning that in the interpretation of Scripture, the *matter* of the Scriptures has an important bearing on the *manner* in which we are to read them. To try to make this clearer, I want to consider a few examples, bearing in mind that this brief book does not cover the whole of biblical interpretation. These show how the varied literary styles in Scripture affects their interpretation. There are books of history, in the sense that they retell what has happened in the life of Israel or of the early church. This is not secular history, or it is not altogether, for it ascribes certain events directly to God, who is throughout regarded as the God of Israel, who is wholly unlike the gods of other nations, the Creator and Lord of the world. Israel are on a course in fulfilment of the terms of God's covenant with Abraham. It is marked by failure and weakness, as well as by faith in the promises and obedience to the divine commands. So this is religious history. It must be borne in mind that the infallibility of the writings is compatible with them containing reports of sin and failure, both national and personal, and the expression of what is untrue.

The Bible is not a collection of romantic tales, where everything turns out for the best, written to make us feel good. The Psalms are a compilation of poetry recounting the writers various states, praise and thanksgiving, fear and penitence, unbelief and fear, what John Calvin referred to as 'the anatomy of all parts of the soul!'[1], as well as recounting many deeds of the Lord in creation, in the life of Israel, and in the Psalmist's life. Several are prophetic, Psalms which during his ministry Jesus took on as being direct references to himself.

In the New Testament, the four Gospels are four overlapping accounts, especially the first three, the synoptic gospels. They have a sequential form, and move from the birth of Jesus, his incarnation, to the agony of the crucifixion and the triumph of the resurrection. Nonetheless they do not all recount the same events. There are differences of emphasis and detail, each being written for a rather different early Christian readership. They are not therefore biographies of Jesus in our sense, but selective, with different emphases. The aim is not to answer every question. In particular the accounts are particularly reticent about the inner consciousness of Jesus. They are not biographies, nor are they autobiographical. They focus on the work that his Father had given him to do. The authors are therefore creative in the sense of being selective. The Acts of the Apostles is the continuation of the Gospel according to Luke, as the early church, in accordance with the promise of Jesus, becomes enlightened and empowered by the descent of the Holy Spirit at Pentecost. Peter refers to the writings of Paul in this vein: 'There are some things in them that are hard to understand, which the ignorant and unstable twist to their own destruction, as they do the other Scriptures' (2 Peter 3:16). We shall have more to say about twisting the Scriptures shortly.

So the infallibility is modulated by the various styles and purposes of the writings.

Of particular importance, of course, is their portrayal of the Lord God himself. He is incomprehensible, as we have already seen. He is infinite and perfect, beyond space and time and so we, finite creatures of space and time, affected by many incapacities and limitations, find him beyond our understanding. This does not mean that his depiction in Scripture is gobble-de-gook. Faced with the various elements of the creation, Job exclaimed 'Behold, these are but the outskirts of his ways, and how small a whisper do we hear of him' (Job 26:16). We cannot get our minds around him to encompass him. At best we can 'apprehend' him. The mystery of his triunity is gradually revealed, not lessened, until its outlines become clearer in the New Testament. The Living God in one God, each of his persons being wholly divine, each distinct from each other. His perfection is celebrated; he is the only object of human worship and unconditional service. His various attributes are recorded, often in the form of 'one-liners' of comment in a narrative. The Bible does not contain a treatise on theology, but God's character is disclosed as part of a narrative, or an account of the Gospel or some other teaching.

THE LORD AND KING HEZEKIAH

Coming to terms with the interactions between the Sovereign Lord and his people requires some care. Consider an Old Testament example of this, God's assertion through his prophet to sickly Hezekiah that he is going to die (Isaiah 38; see also a parallel account in 2 Kings 20). The Lord tells Hezekiah through the prophet Isaiah, 'Set your house in order, for you shall die, you shall not live.' On hearing this he prays to the Lord, weeping and reminding him of his faithfulness. The word of the Lord came again to Isaiah. He is to say to Hezekiah that the Lord will add fifteen years to his life. 'I will deliver you and this city out of the hand of Assyria, and will defend this city' (Isaiah 38:5-6).

How are we to understand this as far as the Bible's overall teaching regarding the unchangeableness of God is concerned? If God is immutable, (as we saw in Hebrews 6 earlier, and as taught throughout Scripture), how can this seeming change of mind concerning Hezekiah's plight be consistent with this? Does the unchanging God change his mind? To answer this question we must first alter the focus of our attention somewhat and consider what the passage as a whole is telling. Is God simply waiting to see how Hezekiah is going to react? What else might he be doing? Well, he might be testing Hezekiah. If he is then what the passage tells us about God is rather different. If Isaiah's first words to Hezekiah are designed as a trial, then what happens subsequently has to be understood differently. These words are not then to be understood as a *prediction*, but as a *test*, as when a mother says to the child teetering near the open fire, 'you will be burned.' These words are not a prediction but a warning. In the same way, in his first words God is not predicting Hezekiah's death but he is testing him. The words are not to be taken in isolation but as part of a wider design. God does not change his mind, as we change ours, but he reveals various possibilities for various times. This is a pattern of divine action, as we can see from the histories of Moses and of Jonah for example.

What this shows, in general terms, is that in our study of the Bible we must attend to the *scope* of the passage. In the Psalms there is repetition, because repetitiveness is how Hebrew poetry was constructed, through the emphasis of repetition. But many passages of the letters of Paul contain dense argument. Think of his letters to the Romans or Galatians or his argument about the resurrection in 1 Corinthians 15. His language needs careful line-by-line study, since every word has significance for his argument. Compare that with the book of Job. Here the focus is much wider. We have to grasp the entire course of Job's trial and only then look at verses in detail. The Ethiopian courtier who we have already met had a *scope question* when he said to Philip 'About whom, I ask you, does the prophet say this, about himself or about someone else' (Acts 8:34)? Philip explained this and much more to him. As a result, the man asked Philip to baptize him, and he went on his way rejoicing.

So as well as studying the Bible's detail, as befits its verbal inspiration, we must change our lens and ask general questions about a book as a whole, or of a particular section. The parts of Paul's writings when he changes from teaching about the destiny of the church to sending greetings to various people are to indicate a different kind of information. If we are coming to a relatively unfamiliar passage of Scripture it may be a good plan to skim it first before studying it in detail. Scripture does not consist only of propositions and assertions, though these are foundational. It also contains questions and commands and covenants and parables. We need to cultivate discipline in our Bible reading, and must resist the temptation of trying to make the Bible say what it does not say, or of giving it a purpose that it does not have. Instead we must concentrate on the 'plot-line' of Scripture.

INFALLIBILITY & FALLIBILITY

The Bible is infallible, but we are fallible. The Bible is infallible, but our understanding is partial and defective, even when we have used every legitimate technique of Bible study. We have intellectual failures, our attention slips, we get tired, we are ignorant of certain things, and we may engage in bad reasoning. We miss the implications of Scripture. There is a marvellous instance of such a hitherto missed implication of Scripture in Christ's debates with the Sadducees, who did not believe in the resurrection of the dead. They tried to trap him with a 'thought experiment' of a man who had seven wives in succession. In the resurrection whose wife will she be? Christ answered them, and then continued:

> And as for the dead being raised, have you not read in the book of Moses, in the passage about the [burning] bush, how God spoke to him, saying "I am the God of Abraham, and the God of Isaac, and the God of Jacob". He is not the God of the dead, but of the living. You are quite wrong.
>
> — MARK 12.26, 27

Who would have thought that the familiar Old Testament teaching, that God is the God of Abraham, Isaac and Jacob, would entail that Abraham is living and that there is to be a resurrection of the dead?

But we face difficulties not only from our ignorance, the failings of our memory, what we don't know, of appreciating the consequences of our what we already believe, though these are significant, but failures of another kind. Paul wrote to the Ephesians, describing them and telling them what he was praying for them. 'Having the eyes of your hearts enlightened, that you may know what is the hope to which he has called you, what are the riches of his glorious inheritance in the saints...' (Ephesians 1:18). Note the emphasis on knowledge. First Paul refers to the eyes of the heart being *enlightened*, which will be the way to *know* what is the hope for a Christian. We have met similar language in 2 Corinthians 4, in connection with the self-authenticating of the Bible.

Why does he pray? Obviously because his Christian hearers cannot bring about these inner changes without the help of God, thinking particularly of God the Holy Spirit. In the previous verse, verse 17, he had asked that they will have 'a spirit of wisdom and of revelation in the knowledge of him'. And that as a result the 'eye of their understanding may be enlightened, that you may what know is the hope to which he has called know you...' and so on.

Familiar words but used in rather unfamiliar, new

circumstances and in different combinations. What are 'the eyes of your hearts?' What the words indicate is that there is in these Ephesians not only ignorance, but resistance to be overcome, and tension to be handled. To know these things will call for fundamental changes in them, in their hearts, their inner selves. They are resistant to such changes; or, more strictly, there is a tension between the desire to know, and a wariness at the cost of such knowledge. This is not simply a case of them adding to the things that they already know about the world round them, but of knowledge of themselves in their relationship to God. They have to change from hostility to worship and service, faith and love, and so to delight. Some things have to be learned, other habits of mind to be unlearned, to be shunned. The knowledge is the sort to re-position the one who knows, to an increasingly appreciative awareness of what it means to be 'in Christ.'

IMPLICIT FAITH

If we stand back from the depths of Paul's prayer to ask what God-given faith and knowledge are like as they grow in answer to a prayer like Paul's, one way of thinking about it is that it is like a web of faith in Scripture. There are other kinds of belief that we have about other matters, about what we are planning for tomorrow or next month or next year, or our beliefs about English history and so on. So perhaps a sheaf of webs! Let's call the web of Joe's convictions about Scripture Joe's web today. At the centre of the web are central matters of the Bible which Joe is convinced of. They are foundational to his outlook as a Christian. Around this central circle of beliefs are those that are important and yet he is resistant to them, because they are matters in conflict with the centre. And then at the outside circle are matters of which he is less and less certain. The circle may be changing shape today to the degree that his beliefs about a matter are currently being reordered.

There are other webs close by. For example there is the web of beliefs not only with respect to whether they are believed strongly or weakly, but whether they are beliefs that are being acted on, put into practice. Of course, we are thinking of webs on the assumption that Joe has good self-knowledge, and this may not be a good assumption in his case. But one thing at a time. Let us assume that he does have good self knowledge. Paul's prayer in Ephesians that we have looked at briefly (the prayer that 'the eyes of their hearts be enlightened') has the intention of reordering the active beliefs of his readers with respect to the work of Christ by fresh appreciations of them, and so enabling them to be more firmly established in their faith. It is easier to have inactive beliefs rather than active ones. This is a plausible understanding of what 'grow in grace and in the knowledge of our Lord Jesus Christ' means.

There is another way of looking at this, which has a

closer bearing on the view of the Scriptures that we have been outlining in this book. A Christian reader of the Bible will have her favourite books, and passages of books. The Gospels, or perhaps one of them; the central letters of Paul—Romans, Galatians, 1 Corinthians. 1 Peter, maybe. But not so Jude, or Revelation, or Philemon, or 2 Corinthians. And in the Old Testament, the Psalms, Genesis, Exodus, 1 Samuel, parts of Isaiah and Jeremiah may be read frequently. But not Leviticus or the books of the Chronicles, or Job, or Obadiah. Why is this? Partly because of the difficulty and obscurity and dryness (or brevity) of some of the books? Perhaps. But also partly, again, because of the recognition of the marginal place that some of them appear to play in revealing the saving purposes of God.

There may seem to be a short step between marginalising some of the ways suggested and denying their canonical status altogether. Why could not everyone come clean and declare the contents of their own personal canon? But this would be a privatizing or subjectivising of Scripture and an undermining of its common objectivity in the church. It is a short step from having a canon of biblical books of one's own to adding to one's list of canonical favourites, perhaps books such as Bunyan's *Pilgrim's Progress* or C.S Lewis's *Screwtape Letters*. But there is another way.

At the time of the Reformation the nature and scope of saving faith was fiercely debated. How is faith to be defined? What is the relation between faith and other graces such as love and hope? There were intense discussions about whether personal faith was implicit or explicit. The idea that one could have a sponsor in the matter of faith in Jesus, leaving such a matter to someone else, the priest or the vicar, while getting on with cultivating one's field or spending time in one's workshop, came to seem preposterous. The Reformers opted for faith as explicit.

But after further thought they came to recognise that there is a legitimate place for implicit faith *along with* the central case of explicit faith. When they read the Gospels they saw that the first disciples of Jesus trusted him while at the same time thinking that some of his teaching was absurd and unsettling, and even wrongheaded. So for example the disciples attempted to prevent Jesus going the way to the Cross (Matthew 16:21). When Jesus dissuaded them, they were then left to await further developments. But though they were extremely puzzled and put out, they did not abandon him. Their faith came to have both explicit and implicit elements. Our faith may be similar. With respect to many matters that are future, we are all in that place of trusting God while also being in a state of ignorance about the many details of his purposes. With respect to obscure and discordant matters it is better that we await more light in a patient frame of mind than pass negative verdicts on unsettling passages of Scripture. Patience is after all a Christian virtue.

There is one last factor that I wish to mention. Many of the New Testament writings were addressed to a church, or to groups of churches. While we may read and study these as individuals, personally, they have a corporate application. We should not do our Bible study in solitary confinement. Paul prays for the believers that 'Christ may dwell in your hearts through faith—that you being rooted and grounded in love, may have strength to comprehend *with all the saints*, what is the breadth and length and height and depth, and to know the love of Christ that surpasses knowledge ...' (Ephesians 3:17-19). Bible study at its best is a corporate activity. This should impact the role our churches give to preaching, small groups and discipleship training.

Confessing the infallibility does not mean that we ought immediately have a firm grasp of every jot and tittle of what part of the Bible we may be reading. If we are puzzled that is not a defect in the text. Understanding may be little by little. None of this affects the truth of the Bible's infallibility.

5. THE BIBLE AND CHRISTIAN DOCTRINE

By now the direction of the arrow is changing significantly. It is turning upwards. We are firmly in the area of 'response', but still with needing the help of God in this. We are beginning to see what is involved in the understanding of Scripture and of what it reveals about God our Creator and Redeemer, and the challenges that this brings. We have got where we are through giving some attention to Scripture's marks as *divine revelation*, *inspired* and *infallible*. In this final chapter we consider more questions about how Scripture should operate in Christian thinking.

Scripture is unique. How is that uniqueness to be retained in Christian activity, in thinking and preaching and teaching and settling questions? How is the church to take forward the content of Scripture? This final chapter is an endeavour to identify some parameters.

The high view of the Bible we have upheld might lead

us to believe that biblicism is the correct approach. Surely we are on safe ground if the ministry of the church were confined to the publication and re-publication of the very words of Scripture, for it is only the very words of Scripture that are inspired and infallible. Won't any other strategy be one of Scripture dilution? On such a strategy, the ministry of the church would then confine itself to the literal reproduction of the text of Scripture. Its publications would be confined to printing portions of biblical texts, its ministry to the verbatim reproduction of texts. That is a policy of *biblicism*.

This may be the safe option, but it is not the Christian option. Think about the following facts. Christ told his first disciples to go into all the world and to preach the gospel, and that they would be divinely supported and empowered in this task. Christ's plan is that his Church be truly international. This is one of the consequences of Christ's coming. The people of God who in the Old Testament were largely confined within the Jewish people were from now onwards to be taken from every nation, thus finally fulfilling the terms of the covenant made with Abraham, that through his seed every nation would be blessed. How is that to be carried forward? Obviously, by translation.

And we have cases of this in the Bible itself. Jesus' natural language was Aramaic. But the documents of the New Testament are in Greek, apart from certain short passages and words that have been retained in their original Aramaic. So already, in the writing of the text of the New Testament, the internationalizing was begun. The legitimacy of this spread was strikingly illustrated by the way in which Jews and others from many different regions heard the wonderful words of the gospel each in their own native tongues on the Day of Pentecost when the Holy Spirit descended with a rushing, deafening sound.

> And at this sound the multitude came together and they were bewildered, because each one was hearing them speak in his own language. And they were amazed and astonished, saying 'Are not all these who are speaking Galileans? And how is it that we hear, each of us in his own native language? Parthians and Medes and Edomites and residents of Mesopotamia, Judea and Cappadocia, Pontus and Asia, Phrygia and Pamphylia, Egypt and the parts of Libya belonging to Cyrene, and visitors from Rome, both Jews and proselytes, Cretans and Arabians—we hear them telling in our own tongues the mighty works of God.
>
> — ACTS 2:6-11

So translation has to be part of the plan, because the Holy Spirit is a translator! And if translation has imperfections, and something is lost in translation, then it is lost when the Holy Spirit translates. And if it is lost when the Holy Spirit translates, whatever that loss means from a literary point of view, it cannot matter as far as transmitting the meaning of Scripture into another language is concerned.

What happens in translation? In a literalistic translation every endeavour is made to keep the meaning of the original. What is lost in translation is the 'aura' of the original, the rhythm of the original words, what they suggest to a native speaker. But such psychological association is not the meaning we are after, otherwise translation would be impossible. To translate 'The window is open' into the French 'La fenêtre est ouverte' loses something, of course, but it preserves much, namely the fact that when it is correct to affirm or deny the first expression, it is correct to affirm or deny the second, and vice versa. Here's another kind of translation, from one literary idiom into another. A parable is a parable, and nothing but a parable is a perfect substitute for it. But a parable can be explained, as Jesus explained the parable of the Sower (Mark 14:13). Does the force of the parable get lost when it is explained? Yes and no. The explanation of a parable is not itself a parable. But the explanation of the parable helps us to understand it, and this is important, because parables were a central part of Jesus' teaching.

Take another example. The apostolic gospel message can be summarised, as in Paul's summary in 1 Corinthians 15:3 onwards: "I delivered to you as of first importance what I also received; that Christ died for our sins in accordance with the Scriptures, that he was buried, that he was raised on the third day in accordance with the Scriptures....' This is the beginning of what Paul ,when writing to Timothy, called a 'form of sound words,' an epitome of the Christian message or of a part of it that was in all likelihood to be remembered and passed on. In these words Paul is not re-enacting the events of the crucifixion and resurrection—it's too late for that—but reporting them in summary form. And such a report is the word of God.

Here are examples of summarizing, extracting and giving the meaning of apostolic teaching, and of sets of events that were included in that teaching. Earlier we stressed the importance of the Bible's history and of its historical trustworthiness, and the New Testament's reliability. Now we are seeing that this is not at odds with important parts of that teaching being 'broken off' or summarized without danger of being misunderstood, and being reissued. This is a part of authentic early church life. The words 'Christ Jesus came into the world to save sinners' first occur in one of Paul's letters, written at a particular time and for a particular purpose. It is a saying that is trustworthy and deserving of full acceptance, Paul says. But Paul is teaching that this saying or assertion or proposition can be taken out of its original context and be 'reissued' in the services and teaching of the Christian church throughout the world and for all time. It is not a timeless saying, because it refers to particular events and definite times, having to do with Jesus' life and ministry, and death and resurrection. Nonetheless it can be reissued for as long as it is efficacious, until the end of time, and in eternity the redeemed saints will celebrate the power of Christ's work by exclaiming, using rather different words, 'Worthy is the Lamb who was slain!' (Revelation 5:12).

In the Old Testament the covenant made with Moses which established Israel in the promised land was a temporary arrangement. God's promises that concerned the land and the people and the worship of Israel were temporary, and have now 'withered away' as the day of the promised Messiah dawned. In the New Testament way of counting, these are the 'last days.' And in them Jesus Christ, by contrast with the temple-centred forms of worship of the Old Testament, is the same yesterday, today and forever, and now the bodies of the faithful are temples.

What we are seeing here (I hope) is the truth of the old saying that *the meaning of Scripture is Scripture.* In biblicism the meaning of Scripture can be nothing other than the very words of Scripture in their original context. But we have seen that this is a position that is unworkable given the mandate of the New Testament itself that the good news is to be taken to the world at large, and that translation was involved in the very production of the four Gospels, for example. The gospel can be summarized and formulated in short statements without its meaning being affected. In any country and in any place it remains true that Jesus came into the world to save sinners. Scripture can be taken from its original context and reissued without any serious loss. In this sense the gospel is timeless. The well-known words of the so-called Apostles Creed, which confesses belief in 'God the Father Almighty...' are likewise in this sense timeless. Having been revealed as God's truth, their truth endures.

This repeated emphasis on meaning is important. The Bible can affect us in all sorts of ways without these being the result of what it means. Suppose I read the parable of the loaves and fishes. Reading it may remind me to go out and to buy the groceries, or it may make me realize that I am in fact hungry. But these effects, each of which may be caused by the reading of a biblical passage, are obviously not part of the passage's meaning, which has to do with Jesus' power and compassion for the multitudes who were at that point listening to him. The meaning of Scripture is central, and anything that reproduces that meaning has the force of Scripture. It does not add to Scripture but it represents or reproduces it.

A THEOLOGICAL BOOK

The Bible, God's book, is a theological book. In education, ours is a day of specialization, and this has affected theological education. There are specialists on the Old Testament, New Testament, Archaeology, Church

History, Philosophy of Religion, Biblical Theology and so on in a way that was not the case in the past. This has advantages in that intense attention can be devoted to one subject. Bookshelves groan. But the overall effect is to break up the Bible into different bits which are of significance to each specialism. So there may be concentration on, say, the theology of Peter, which becomes a different area of specialization from the theology of Paul. And the idea that Paul's letter to the Romans, for example, is to be regarded as raw research data that we should be encouraged to read with fresh eyes, is surely a mistake. The idea that the Bible presents an overall picture of anything theological, in particular a doctrine of God, has become, strangely, of secondary interest, a kind of interdisciplinary project for which there is little enthusiasm. Such a synoptic view of the Bible, in which the sixty-six books are in effect treated as one book, is thought to be anachronistic.

But this approach is seriously defective. In looking at the various elements the whole picture is compromised. And if we are not careful, the Bible as a devotional aid becomes substantially smaller than the revealed 66 book canon that is the Bible. The historic position has been that the Bible, being inspired, is a unique book and its main spine, its core, is intelligible to the non-specialist. It does not require a 'priesthood' to interpret it. It can be read as literature, or as a book that throws light on the ancient Middle East, but these activities are of secondary importance. What is of prime importance is its overall teaching, open to all and sundry.

If the accurate translation of the Bible into another language, or its summarizing, preserves its status as the word of God, then this also has an important bearing on preaching and teaching. If preaching is the exposition of a passage or theme of Scripture, and its application to a congregation, then this has serious implications. A sermon is not to be like an after-dinner speech, or a time when the speaker lets off steam, but it is the word of God! Being a talk at a certain point in a service does not make it the word of God, nor does praying before a person speaks make it special, but the words being a rehearsing of the themes of Scripture is what matters. In tackling such a theme, the speaker is bringing the word of God to the people, and applying it to them. And being a herald of the word of God is a serious business, don't you think?

The Christian reader of Scripture not only considers its themes, but the way in which the Bible records the development of a doctrine. In the matter of the doctrine of God, it developed over the eras of revelation. In this way the doctrine of God has features that God himself does not have. So the doctrine of God has grown from being the revelation of God to Abraham, then to Moses, to David, to Isaiah, and finally through his Son and his early disciples. The idea of 'augmentation' is key. The various names given to God in the early days in which God revealed himself indicate different features of God's character. These differences complement each other, they do not conflict or contradict. The Lord our God is one Lord.

A similar point applies to the various authors. Paul refers almost habitually to the church as a 'body', the 'body of Christ', on occasion working out that figure in considerable detail (1 Corinthians 12), but Peter says nothing like this, instead referring to the church as a priesthood and a nation (1 Peter 2:9) and elsewhere as 'pilgrims' or 'sojourners.' These differences do not imply that the apostolic teaching is at odds with itself. Rather the conclusion we should draw is that there are more than one or two ways in which the church can be described, each description being qualified by the other. This is particularly important when figures of speech are used. The fact that the Bible is presupposed to be one book, and the church of Christ as one church, warrants a harmonising way of interpreting the varied references to it. And similarly with other themes. Harmonising is a crucial assumption for those who wish to submit to the authority of all Scripture, rightly understood.

So these differences are not discordances, or contradictions. A person may have different qualities which are identified by his various friends and acquaintances. Some are more displayed in the family, others by near friends, some may be seen at work, others at home. These may be had by one and the same person. Of course in the case of a human being it is possible to be all things to all other people. A person's private life may be at odds with his public image.

But with God such a mismatch is inconceivable. The development in understanding, if it keeps within the contours of Scripture, may be thought of as revealing different aspects of his purposes and his powers in relation to his people and to the wider creation. This process has to do both with what was necessary in a given era, and with what the people could 'bear.' Often these developments may seem incidental to the narrative. At one point a biblical writer may note that God is the 'judge of all', interjecting this in a narrative unselfconsciously, at other times the 'doctrine of God' as we call it is set forth more formally, as with the famous self-disclosure to Moses at the burning bush. Moses asks:

> If I come to the people of Israel and say to them, 'The God of your fathers has sent me to you' and they ask me; 'What is his name?' what shall I say to them?' God said to Moses, "I AM WHO I AM". And he said "Say this to the people of Israel, 'I AM has sent me to you'".... 'This is my name for ever, and thus I am to be remembered throughout all generations.'
>
> — EXODUS 3:13-15

Interestingly, here the Lord stresses that this oneness is fundamental to his name, his character, and is to endure in the history of Israel and beyond. The God of the fathers of Israel is henceforward to be regarded as 'I AM', which emphasizes the unique unity and self-existence of God.

The revelation in Scripture progresses, that is, it is augmented, the later building on the earlier, looking back on it and evaluating and estimating its significance. What Jesus says about Israel's past, in some cases leaving its effects behind and in other cases deepening it, for example in the ways he says 'You have hear that it was said... but I say to you...' (e.g. Matthew 5:38f), is to deepen such points and at the same time to exercise his authority over his disciples. He does this in foretelling the destruction of Jerusalem, the centre of Jewish worship and culture, and how he viewed the Roman occupation of his day. He deals with the significance of places in worship: the time is coming when men should worship the Father in spirit and truth (John 4:27). The Letter to the Hebrews and Paul's Letter to the Galatians are particularly important regarding what is now outdated, but mandatory in the Old Testament. They set out clearly and unmistakably what in a particular past era is left behind, but not to be forgotten totally. The typological and anticipatory character of the God-given sacrificial system pertained to the state of the people of God as children, who reach adulthood with the coming of Christ (Galatians.4:1 f). But the continuing importance of the moral law, the Decalogue, and of the piety of the OT saints, to whom the promises are central (Hebrews 11) is upheld. The new order is one which centres on the coming city which has foundations, the Jerusalem 'from above,' whose maker and keeper is God, and the people of God as a pilgrim people. So the relationship between the Old and New Testaments is a rather complex one in which some elements are left behind and some deepened in accordance with Old Testament prophecies in Jeremiah and Isaiah about the day of the coming of the Messiah.

Among the various ways of summarising the Bible is the making of Christian doctrine, biblical synopses of a particular matter. This is the bringing together of biblical data on the matter concerned in various themes and emphases. It is important to remember that these doctrines have often been formed as the result of controversy within and at the borders of the Christian church, particularly in the early church and at the period of the Reformation and immediately after.

The Bible is a theological book in two senses. It is full of theological matter, and it is above all the book which has central to it the revealed account of the saving purposes of the God and Father of our Lord Jesus Christ. 'For from him and through him and to him are all things. To him be glory for ever. Amen' (Romans 11:36).

DEFENDING THE FAITH

In defending and articulating the faith Christians are faced with a dilemma. Here the biblicism that we discussed earlier is clearly not enough. The deviations from and oppositions to the biblical account of the faith have to be responded to in the terms in which the deviations are expressed, otherwise minds can never be properly engaged in debate and discussion. So in the so-called Patristic era words in Scripture are given new precision, and words that are not in Scripture but in the general culture, and which are used by those who question the faith at some point become of importance. In debates regarding the Trinity (not itself a biblical word, remember) and regarding the person of Christ, words such as *substance*, *essence*, and *person* are introduced, and biblical words such as *nature* (e.g. Romans 1:20) are refined in the light of the controversies. In the Reformation, the Reformed and Protestant side took on the scholastic language of late medievalism in terms such as *accident* or *habit*, to debate with the theologians not only about the character of the Lord's Supper, but about the nature of faith and justification, about merit and good works, about the grace of God in the soul, and the church and its ministry.

But isn't using this new language, new concepts, in controversy, given what we have been insisting is the verbal inspiration of Scripture, dangerous? Most certainly.

Great care is needed. And so we need to remind ourselves of some matters that we discussed earlier.

We have already underlined that the meaning of Scripture is Scripture. Christian doctrine can only be stated, and deviations from it discussed, given this principle. We have also seen that the principle is in fact inevitable. But we must be wary of a mistaken *creativity* and of *speculation*.

Second, in controversies the sole authority of Scripture in matters of faith must be maintained. This places on Christian controversy the obligation to return to Scripture at every step. There must be a process of visiting and revisiting Scripture, of iteration, to establish that the position reflects what is revealed and only that and that this revelation actually bears on what is controverted. There must be a willingness to take difficulties and deviations seriously. This consulting of Scripture is not without precedent. There are biblical examples of this happening. When the Bereans heard the apostles, they searched the Scriptures to see whether what they said was so (Acts 17:11). There are instances of the apostles as a body having to deal with new circumstances, as in the Council of Jerusalem (Acts 15).

Thirdly, we must bear in mind the overall purpose of revelation, which is not to provide answers to all our questions, but to make the readers of Scripture 'wise for salvation' (2 Timothy 3:16). Tensions can arise in our minds at this point between the desire to study a topic further and further in order to be clear, and the demands of discipleship, which may be more 'practical' in the sense that the Christian faith is not simply a matter of intellectual interest (though it does have this side). The needs of discipleship require that the faith should be applicable to the tasks of living. Yet we must be careful not to treat matters of truth simply pragmatically.

Can we manage without controversy? Not really. There is a strand of New Testament teaching that false teaching is permitted in order to sift the genuine from the false disciple (e.g. 1 Corinthians 11:17). It is good if controversy can be managed in a civilised and friendly way, and not result in the violence that has occasionally disfigured the church's past. The days of the rack and the thumbscrew are happily no longer present! But this does not mean that doctrinal controversy no longer matters, or that the differences between groups are insignificant. The toleration of many views in society is not the same thing as it not mattering which view is held by the Church. Does freedom of speech mean that nothing matters any longer? That would be absurd. And we need to remember that many of our freedoms are not present in other societies, and people in them, including Christians, routinely suffer for professing their faith publicly. 'We must remember those that are in prison, as though in prison with them' (Hebrews 13:3).

DOES DOCTRINE DEVELOP?

Behind the issue of controversy there is another question looming, that of whether doctrine develops. The idea of development is itself slippery. A small tumour may develop into a larger tumour. That is obviously not a welcome development. There are developments in society which are benign, and others which are malign. Nothing but confusion can result from ignoring this distinction and assuming that change is always change for the better, or for the worse.

Due to cultural changes in society, including changes in people's religious outlook, particular passages of the Bible may become worn smooth, or disregarded. In such circumstances Christians may think it is necessary to make the original meaning plain. The original meaning may have to be explained, and then applied to the Christian community or to Christians within it, for above all things the divine revelation should be understood. To understand a writing involves also being able to say what that writing does *not* mean. And this is true of the meaning of the Bible. It is in such circumstances that theological and religious developments occur.

In the nineteenth century, in a book that became well known, *An Essay on the Development of Christian Doctrine* (1846), Cardinal John Henry Newman spelled out what he proposed as a doctrine of development. Newman's idea was that if a mind is steeped in the thought of God, of

Christ, and of the Holy Spirit, if these become the object of attention, this will naturally result in the desire to form statements about them, one statement leading to another, fresh evolutions occurring from the original idea. This process is the 'development' of the idea, and it results in a series of dogmatic statements. And this is what has happened, Newman thought, in the Christian Church.

But what sort of control is there over the course of such developments? Does any evolution count as legitimate? That would hardly be a satisfactory proposal. How does healthy growth differ from cancerous growth? Newman went on to suggest a series of 'notes' or tests which developments must meet if they are to be valid and wholesome. So, he said, these evolutions in thought are rather like the growth of a tree or other organism. Of course, it is possible to distinguish a diseased tree from a healthy tree, a sound from a malformed specimen, and so on. There are recognized, objective tests which can be applied. But whether there are similar tests for doctrinal development is precisely what is at issue. What would a healthy doctrinal development be, and what counts as a malformation? The fact that the development has 'naturally' occurred, whatever precise conditions have led to it, does not mean that the development is valid or wholesome, or that it is in accordance with biblical revelation and its role within the church.

We have stressed that the meaning of Scripture is Scripture. And so a test of development that is closer to

the teaching of the revelation must be one that preserves
the meaning of Scripture in new circumstances. In an era
before Newman, in the seventeenth century, the
Westminster Confession advanced the following proposal:
that we are to take as our authority what is 'expressly set
down in Scripture, or by good and necessary consequence
may be deduced from Scripture' (Westminster Confession
1:4). This reminds us that the meaning that the Scriptures
have is linguistic meaning, the meaning that statements
and assertions and questions and commands have. It is
not meaning or significance in a wider sense, as when we
say that clouds mean rain, or that what has happened
means trouble.

What the Westminster Confession proposed is that
we retain the meaning of Scripture, and thus its authority,
not only when we study the very words of Scripture, but
also when we deduce other words from them. So the vital
question is what the words of Scripture imply, not what
they suggest. As noted earlier, what the words of
Scripture suggest to me may be different from what they
suggest to you, which is hopeless for retaining the
authority of Scripture. Earlier we noted the fact that the
term 'Trinity' is not in Scripture. But the church has
found it to be a legitimate derivation from scriptural data
on God the Father, God the Son and God the Holy Spirit.
Each is the same unique, one God. So God is three and
God is one. One in *substance*, three in his *persons*. So the
sense of the way in which the Trinity is one is different

from that in which the Trinity is three. This great mystery of the godhead is at the centre of our faith. This Trinitarian proposal has been debated and discussed and has stood the test of time, and hence it is judged to be a valid inference from the data of Scripture.

The phrase we quoted from the Confession includes the word *good*: 'good and necessary consequence.' This, I think, is a reference to how we understand a passage of Scripture. For example, the Bible refers to the fingers of God and his feet. But it is not a necessary consequence of such expressions in Scripture that God has a body and therefore dwells in a particular location. These conclusions are not warranted. Why? Because other parts of Scripture teach that God is spirit (John 4:24) and that he is immeasurable, and so on. So we must conclude that the references to feet, or to fingers, or to breath, are figurative or metaphorical references. It is not safe to draw inferences about how God really is from them. Such inferences would not be 'good.'[1]

Before we conclude this discussion we must note a final problem. We have been discussing how the Scripture is to be interpreted. Suppose we are agreed on that. Such agreement does not settle what we may call the *scope* of the Scriptures, the limits of what it relates to. Here the question is, in the work and organisation of the church, is the rule, *only what Scripture commands* is to be our guide, or *what the Scripture does not forbid* is to be our guide? Does the silence of Scripture on a matter imply that it is forbidden, or does the fact that the Bible does not rule a matter out mean that it is permissible? Some churches such as the Lutheran and the Anglican, have historically taken the wider position, while others, such as Congregational and Presbyterian, have taken the narrower. This is an important difference about the scope of the Scripture.

Whichever view is taken, it is undoubtedly the case that in churches traditions have grown up, ways of doing things that Christians do not question and may cling to. A tradition simply means what has been handed down. Paul, for example, received and in turn handed down the apostolic teaching about Jesus' death and resurrection; this is the receiving and handing on of the word of God. Traditions can be good or bad; and their usefulness may change with time. Some of the things that get decided and handed down may act like barnacles on the hull of a boat. The preface to the *Book of Common Prayer* warns that no tradition has been devised 'by the wit of man' that it has not in due course of time 'been corrupted.' Jesus recognised how the Pharisees for the sake of their traditions 'made void the word of God,' stifling its voice (Matthew 15:1-9). So in all churches there have grown up ways of doing things which have a tendency to choke God's Word. We all have a role to play in working to ensure with care that we are hearing God's Word aright, and allowing it to correct our traditions, wrong beliefs and assumptions.

A WORD IN CONCLUSION

The last phase of our discussion may have seemed a bit negative. If so, this is unfortunate. God's Word is the greatest treasure we have and it brings joy, life and peace (Psalm 19). We ought to end on a positive note!

In this short book we have come a long way in a short space. In closing, in the midst of all the matters we have touched on, it is important to thank God for the Bible itself. God's gift of the Bible means we are not reduced to 2,000 years of Chinese whispers, or mere fragments of what history has been preserved of any apostolic writing. We have learned that in the providence of God's grace, the Bible is an intrinsic part of God's coming down to us. Thank God for the downward arrow. Without the Saviour, we are of all people the most miserable. And thank God for turning the arrow around, for enabling lives of faithful Christian discipleship through joyful belief and obedience to his authoritative word.

NOTES

2. The Bible's Authority

1. The second chapters of I Corinthians ought to be read in full to get a full impression of what Paul means by 'glory', and the contrast between the 'power' and 'weakness', and 'wisdom' and 'foolishness' of the Gospel in contrast with the usual human estimates of these. This theme continues and is amplified in Paul's second letter to Corinth. For a helpful study of this see J. I. Packer, *Weakness is the Way*.

2. These matters are covered with clarity and brevity in the relevant articles appended to the ESV Study Bible (2008). More detail can be found in Chapters 11 & 15 of The Enduring Authority of the Christian Scriptures (Ed. D. A. Carson), 2016.

3. Objectivity

1. They are quoted not to show the place of the Word of God in Barth's overall theology, but simply to illustrate a kind of thinking. They are taken from his *Church Dogmatics* II.I. p.507 of the English translation.

4. Infallibility

1. See John Calvin's Preface to his commentary on the Psalms.

5. The Bible and Christian doctrine

1. For a helpful, brief treatment of this issue, see *Good and Necessary Consequence,* Ryan M. McGraw, (Grand Rapids, Reformation Heritage Books), 2012.